Easy Gardening

NO STRESS—NO STRAIN

JACK KRAMER

FULCRUM PUBLISHING

Golden, Colorado

Copyright © 1991 Jack Kramer

Book Design by Ann E. Green
Cover Photograph Copyright © 1991 Photo/Nats

Library of Congress Cataloging-in-Publication Data

Kramer, Jack, 1927–
    Easy gardening : no stress—no strain / Jack Kramer — [Updated and
expanded ed.]
      p.   cm.
    Rev. ed. of : Gardening without stress and strain. 1973.
    ISBN 1-55591-083-1
    1. Gardening. I. Kramer, Jack, 1927–   Gardening without stress
and strain. II. Title.
    SB453.K716   1991
    635—dc20   90–85220
                                          CIP

Printed in the United States of America

0 9 8 7 6 5 4 3 2 1

Fulcrum Publishing
350 Indiana Street
Golden, Colorado 80401

CONTENTS

Dig It! ... But Easily

In the beginning if people would have told me I would be an avid gardener for twenty years I would have laughed at them. Yet, here I am today (after having gardens in Illinois and Florida), gardening in California and writing about it. Through the years there have been several changes in my gardening practices; I have devised easier methods, some tricks and shortcuts which allow me to garden without undue stress or strain.

This book is about the changes I have adopted in my garden methods, the shortcuts and trial-by-experience methods I have learned to keep on my feet and off my knees and still tend a garden. Indeed, as one grows older the pleasures of a garden become more important than in former years. So no matter what your age or physical limitations, there are ways to garden, and that is what this book is all about.

I rely heavily on raised and elevated post gardens, outdoor container gardens, and in winter a fine indoor greenery. I employ natural controls such as birds and insects to keep the garden healthy so I don't have to mix, prepare, and spray dubious chemicals, and I use composts to maintain a rich soil and mulches to keep weeds away. I also believe in planning and planting the natural or informal garden, which requires little work compared to the formal landscape.

Gardening without stress or strain involves more brain power than muscle power; learn how to get things done for you but always maintain absolute control. Keep your fingers in the soil but don't throw your back out of place. Exercise is important, but you must realize your limitations. Dig it, but easily. Plant it, but well. And tend it always, with love.

—Jack Kramer

CHAPTER ONE

It's All in the Planning

Over a period of fifteen years I started three gardens of my own; each site presented different gardening problems at different ages in my life. The first garden I literally dug myself. I was young—so was my back—and the only fatality was a bee sting. I planned the second garden completely on paper, but I didn't do all the digging. I had helpers. For my present garden I planned it first on paper and consulted a landscape contractor. As a result of good planning, there was very little hard digging and spading but still enough physical labor to provide suitable exercise for me. Thus, this third method is the ideal one because it makes gardening easier for mind and body and saves money. It is much less trouble to follow a sketch and know where you're going than to pull up trees and shrubs or replant and do needless work.

Plan the garden slowly, and let the idea simmer a few days. Don't be afraid to seek professional help. A consultation or two with a landscaper will help you get started and then you can take it over. (And do take over since it is *your garden!*) These meetings should not be expensive—generally no more than $25 to $50 per meeting. But before you do anything, study garden catalogs because they are helpful if you know how to judge their value.

GARDEN CATALOGS

Garden catalogs are enjoyable to read during dreary winter days. But don't just browse; make notes as you read (if you have gardened for many years you'll be doing this anyway). Some of the best catalogs on my desk and always at my elbow are those of *Wayside Gardens, Whiteflower Farm Gardens, Park Seed,* and *Burpee.*

The author's terrace garden was planned and built so bending and stooping to tend plants is at a minimum. Paths are carefully planned to allow easy access to the terraces. (Photo by author)

(There are other good ones, but these are the ones I have worked with for years.)

When you read your catalogs, keep in mind the plant categories: perennials, annuals, bulbs, trees, and shrubs. (I'm sure you already know some of them.) It helps greatly to know plant names so you can plan your garden intelligently. If the Latin names of plants seem ponderous, keep at it; eventually you'll become acquainted with more plants than you ever thought possible. (Remember you have all winter to do it.) Knowing the correct name of a plant means you will get the plant you want.

Don't let glorious color photographs mislead you and cause visions of grandeur. It takes several years to attain the garden of your dreams, but patience is a virtue of age. That perfect garden is possible, but it takes time, planning, and work (money, too, I might add).

Do make lists of what you think you want; for example, perennials and annuals. But remember that trees and shrubs are the most important items, so study them long and hard. They are the backbone of a garden.

LANDSCAPE HELP

Few professional landscape architects will handle a small, private residential site, but a good landscape contractor, planner, or garden consultant will. Ask contractors by phone just how well acquainted they are with local plant material. This is essential. You will already have some idea of what you want in the way of arrangement in the garden because you have looked over catalogs, and studied books and sketches.

Ask consultants just what their fees are before they make a visit. Ask whether their fees include a sketch plan or merely conversation, and take it from there. Be honest and tell them you want their help to start and do not necessarily want a finished plan at the moment.

You can find these professional helpers listed in the phone book under nurseries, landscape consultants, and so forth. If that approach isn't successful, consult your local newspapers' classified ads. Beware of magazine ads that offer landscape assistance in the form of brochures, booklets, and schooling practices. Some of these services may be perfectly worthwhile, but I always find it wise to deal with people in my own area because they know the local flora best.

The author's box garden on a deck; in such planters plants are easy to weed and cultivate, and bending is virtually eliminated. (Photo by author)

Take your time and select the expert that will do the most for you (but not necessarily for the least money). You are seeking knowledge and service; make sure you get it.

DON'T DO TOO MUCH TOO FAST

Once you have studied garden catalogs and books and have planned your garden on paper with or without professional help, don't rush into the garden and start digging. You want exercise, but gardening that has to be replaced is needless exercise. It is better to take your time and avoid a sprained muscle.

When the plan is finished and you are satisfied with it, decide just whom you can hire to do the job best. At this point if you say "No one can work in my garden as I do," I certainly won't dispute that. But for major construction jobs, younger people can do a better job than you. If there are beds to dig and spading to be done, you can, of course, do some, but for most muscle work hire helpers.

Local nurseries or classified ads list services. But again, be sure you get someone familiar with the terrain. And it is not a question of professional help but rather of getting someone willing to do hard work. Indeed, professional gardeners are scarce these days and, if located, expensive.

If you can, get some local high school students, even if it means telling them step by step what to do. Eventually they'll do it right and save you the backbreaking job of establishing the garden. There will be plenty of time to garden once things are established (or, at any rate, well under way). Seeds and perennials, bulbs and annuals are going to be with us a long time—make sure you don't hurry so you'll be around to enjoy the garden. Lay the framework first.

Once the soil is prepared to your liking (this is discussed in Chapter 3), walk your property several times to decide just where you want fences, patios, and so on; it is easier to install them now rather than later. Don't let a fence throw you; there are innumerable designs available free for the asking from various wood companies.

Don't be afraid to poke around in other people's gardens to see what grows in your neighborhood. This is a grand way to avoid growing what you don't like. But don't snoop deliberately; ask first to see the garden. You'll get much information and misinformation. Just how to separate the two is a challenge, but even if you don't garner any good ideas you'll make some new friends.

If all else fails, and you can't find a local garden consultant, call the local college or botanical gardens, explain your situation, and ask some questions. People at these places are always more than willing to help. Don't ask them to plan your garden; keep your questions simple: which plants will or will not grow in your area.

CHAPTER TWO

Tools and Special Aids

I think we all—young and old—pretty much realize that having the proper tools and aids (and all in *one* place) for a job is half the battle of gardening. It saves wear and tear on the muscles and needless swearing—you can conserve your energy for the actual gardening job. But there are so many different kinds of hand tools—hoes and rakes, spades and shovels—that selecting the right type almost becomes a paramount problem. And the right decision is necessary; when a long-handled shovel splits in two in a youngster's hand there is little physical damage, but in less agile hands it could mean broken bones.

There is also an endless selection of power tools. In fact, there are so many, from electric hedge clippers to lawn vacuum machines, that garden magazines devote pages to them yearly. However, you can skip these pages since you need only a few important power tools (which we shall discuss in a later section).

Greenhouses are, of course, not an essential part of gardening, but they are a great convenience in many ways. In them you can start plants, sow seeds, start cuttings, harden plants, and so forth, without ever bending! That alone makes a small greenhouse essential for me. (See Chapter 11 for a more detailed discussion of these useful structures.) Finally, there are also garden helpers that you yourself can make and special aids that make gardening more enjoyable.

HOES, RAKES, AND OTHER HAND TOOLS

There are many kinds of hoes; a few are indispensable because of their usefulness. For example, a hoe takes the bending out of

Tree cutting shears are easy to use and should be part of the gardener's tool kit. (Photo by Matthew Barr)

weeding, and although you can't get out all of the weeds with a hoe, you can, after some experience, get most of them. Hoes are also good for breaking up dry soils and making furrows. You really don't need the standard, wide-bladed, and scuffle hoes, but definitely get a weeding hoe and a Warren hoe because they are great labor savers. What brand you buy depends on what is available in your local area, but do buy the best you can afford. And remember to *hold* the hoe first; the weights of hoes vary and the length of the handle should suit your body stature.

Rakes are more important than most people think. (By the way, raking the garden of debris and lawn clippings and smoothing the soil is fine exercise for almost everyone.) I have several—leaf, iron-pronged, grass, self-cleaning, pronged, and spading rakes (and no doubt a few more I have forgotten)—because they have innumerable uses. I use a level-headed iron rake for breaking up soil and a springy bow rake for cleaning debris. Avoid bamboo rakes since they are troublesome and invariably break after a few months of use. I find the iron-pronged rake is good for breaking up hard soil and for light weeding and cultivating jobs. Once again, buy the best you can afford, and look for good balance and heavy-duty materials.

Although you might think you won't be using spades and shovels, there will be times when even your most trusted helpers just don't do what you want them to and you will be pressed into service. The most useful shovels include the round-headed and square-bladed; the helpful spades are the trench, regular, narrow, and small. When making your selection, keep in mind that shovels and spades are designed for scooping, digging, lifting, and mixing

A wood saw can be used to prune small branches; seal wounds afterwards with proper sealants. (Photo by Seymour Smith & Sons)

A small hand clipper like this SNAP CUT is handy for many garden chores. (Photo by Seymour Smith & Sons)

soils. I use only a round-pointed shovel for digging and a square or regular spade for adding soil amendments, turning soil, and sometimes even for weeding. The handles of shovels and spades are long, short, or shaped like a "D"; use the shape that is most comfortable.

Generally hand trowels are pointed, rounded, or flat-edged, scoop- or spatula-shaped. Buy a *sturdy* trowel since working hard soil will bend shanks on all but the best, and select a well-balanced trowel that fits your hand.

Pruning tools, too, come in a variety of models; there are border, grass, pruning, and lopping shears, to mention some. There are also hedge shears (four different kinds), pruning saws (four different kinds), and pole saws (two different kinds). Confusing, isn't it? Well, let's simplify it. Although I have purchased many pruning tools in twenty years of gardening, I only use three kinds. I have a small pruning shears; this is the basic pruning tool for countless light cutting jobs. I also use a lopping shears more than I thought I would; this has a long handle and gives you more cutting strength than one-hand shears. I use this tool to cut small limbs, branches, etc. My third tool is a pruning saw, used to cut small limbs and branches.

Pole pruners and pole saws for sawing branches high overhead should be avoided. Cutting trees with these long-handled gadgets is not wise. There is just too much of a chance for accidents. Hedge and border shears, I suppose, are necessary to some people but I have never had occasion to use them. I manage fine with my small pruning shears.

Note that all tools should be kept clean and free of rust—after using tools always wipe away soil and dry any metal parts. Occasionally oil tools to keep them in tiptop shape.

POWER TOOLS

This section is purposely short because power tools, although designed for convenience and labor saving, are difficult to operate and store, and are costly. As mentioned, a few power tools are vital to the gardener, but most aren't. Forget cleaning machines, garden tillers, tractors, chain saws, and elaborate electric mowers. Probably all you really need is a cordless electric hedge-and-shrub trimmer and maybe a lightweight electric garden vacuum, which saves much labor. So don't let glitter and gleam tempt you; use your good judgment and buy only what you need.

MY GARDEN HELPER

It has been said that a little bending never hurt anyone. This is *generally* true, but for people with back trouble bending is a difficult task. A few years ago I visited several lumber companies—I wanted something that would relieve the strain on my back muscles and hold both my tools and me when my hands had to be near the soil for weeding and planting. (I had tried a wooden stool, but invariably I had to run back and forth for tools.) The solution was a low bench (12 inches high and 18 inches across) that I built to enable me to be seated next to the ground I was working. I put my tools in storage bins in the sides of the bench. This portable bench was equipped with ball casters so it could be moved easily without lifting it.

SPECIAL AIDS

Because you will be handling soil, rocks, weeds, and sometimes thorny plants, a good pair of gloves is a must. Cloth and plastic gloves are useful, but unfortunately they usually come in only two sizes: large or small, so get leather gloves—they are available in several sizes. Make sure the gloves don't slip from the hands and that they aren't too tight.

I used to scoff at the idea of kneepads, but I don't any more. When I must kneel, I find that the foam-rubber kneepads (sold at nurseries) are quite comfortable and save the knees from stone bruises and unnecessary pavement attacks. Shop before you buy though, and pick the pads that tie securely in place; some kneepads are impossible to tie and end up around your ankles, which is hardly good for gardening!

Try to obtain a carpenter's apron for wear in the garden. This handy piece of clothing has pockets and loops for tools. It has saved me much walking; I can carry shears, fertilizer packets, and an assortment of things I always seem to need while gardening. Some lumber stores sell carpenter's aprons, but most don't. Nevertheless, keep searching—they are well worth the effort.

A wheelbarrow should not be a special aid; it is really a necessity in a garden and I use it for numerous things. I haul soil in it, move plants in it, mix cement in it, and generally use it whenever I want to carry things and not lift them. By all means buy the best wheelbarrow you can afford. There are three or four models in several price brackets. Two of the less expensive wheelbarrows lasted exactly three months before the wheel gave way and was unrepairable. My expensive wheelbarrow ($59.50) has served me for eight years now.

A friend suggested another useful device for gardening, a miner's or camper's pick. This simple tool can be used for a multitude of garden chores: digging, spading, weeding, chopping, and cultivating. It should be called the gardener's friend but unfortunately is not available at garden stores. You'll find it in surplus stores that carry camping and hiking gear. Get one and try it. I think you'll agree with me that it is an indispensable garden aid.

WATERING AND DRIP-SYSTEM WATERING

Water is the lifeline of a plant, and it must reach plant roots in sufficient quantity. Don't think you can keep your garden growing by hand sprinkling a few minutes a day—it won't work.

Even though completely automatic watering devices are wonderful, some people can't afford them, so you may have to rely on sprinklers or hoses. But be careful—I have a friend who is constantly running back and forth adjusting sprinklers and invariably getting drenched. He ends the day totally exhausted! This is not the way to water plants unless you are racing toward a heart attack.

In addition, if you are watering your plants with conventional hoses or sprinklers, you are wasting water because only a minute percentage of water from sprinklers and hoses reaches plant roots. The rest is wasted runoff. And plants never really grow—they merely exist. Many gardeners overwater plants and waste water by using standard hoses.

Drip systems, however, deliver a specific amount of water directly to plant roots, and in drought areas of the United States applying only what a plant needs in moisture is a very important factor. Wasting our water supply must be stopped. Let's look at a few alternative watering methods.

Watering with Hoses

It may take water from a hose an hour to penetrate 24 inches into the soil. Because most plants, trees and shrubs especially, have roots far below the surface of the soil, you may have to stand and hose down the area almost all day to have the moisture reach the plants' roots. Consider the penetration times shown here:

Soil Depth	Coarse Sand	Sandy Loam	Clay Loam
12 inches	15 minutes	30 minutes	60 minutes
24 inches		60 minutes	
30 inches	40 minutes		
48 inches	60 minutes		

Obviously, hoses are not a desirable watering method.

Watering with Sprinklers

Portable sprinklers are a bother; they invariably have to be moved at inconvenient times to different areas (unless you purchase several of them), and generally can only deliver water in a 7- to 9-foot radius. Permanent buried sprinkler systems deliver water to an overall area—they water everything in their path, not just plants that need moisture. Much of the water may evaporate into the air or run off the surface of the soil into gutters and ditches, especially in clay or hard soil. Also, it seems that most sprinklers break down after a short time (my experience anyway), and although some do a better job than others, sprinklers do waste water in the long run.

However, if you are unable to afford a more expensive system, sprinklers may serve as a functional watering system. Because there are so many kinds of sprinklers, do some investigation before you buy one. You want one that will save you work and time. Once placed, it should stay put so that all you have to do is go out once and turn on the faucets.

I took a lesson from the highway planting department and invested in what is known as a Rain Bird. This unit throws water at great velocity in a circular pattern. It will take a few trial runs before you find the right place for the Rain Bird, a place where it is "raining" on the right amount of the property. But once in place the "bird" can be left and turned on with a flick of the hand.

Another type of watering device is the oscillating sprinkler, which throws water in alternating waves from side to side; this provides soil with a thorough soaking without forming puddles on the ground. These devils, though, are rather difficult to set because they have a hand-operated control that reads "left," "right," or "center" and only approximates where the water is to fall. But like the Rain Bird, the oscillating sprinkler can be left in place.

Depending on the size of your property, you will need one, two, or more sprinklers. I have almost a half acre of three gardens and I use four sprinklers: two oscillating types and two Rain Birds, which seems to work fine.

Hoses (used to deliver water to sprinklers) are another vital part of gardening, although they may not seem so when you start to move them around. Today, thanks to American ingenuity, there are many kinds of hoses, but basically the old-fashioned types are still the only good ones. The plastic hose, unless handled with great care, and the flat hose invariably wiggle around. Buy a good, sturdy rubber hose. It will last and last, is easily handled, and can be mistreated and pushed around without undue damage.

Unfortunately, water pressure fluctuates within a sprinkler, and the area moistened can receive erratic watering. To see this, set an empty coffee can in the area of your plants, turn on the sprinklers and note how long it takes (hours) for the can to fill up with water. Sprinklers waste water because it runs downhill into gutters and ditches. Plants can be in danger of perishing from lack of moisture.

Underground emitters

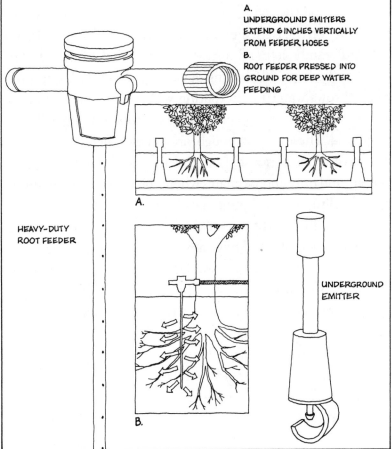

A.
UNDERGROUND EMITTERS
EXTEND 6 INCHES VERTICALLY
FROM FEEDER HOSES

B.
ROOT FEEDER PRESSED INTO
GROUND FOR DEEP WATER
FEEDING

HEAVY-DUTY
ROOT FEEDER

A.

B.

UNDERGROUND
EMITTER

(Drawing by Michael Valdez)

Watering with Drip Systems

As an alternative, drip systems and emitters in proper places allow water to reach plant roots, with little or none wasted, and plants grow at a steady pace. If your garden is on a slope or a terraced arrangement, drip-system watering is the only practical answer. It

Drip emitters

REED IN-LINE EMITTER

REED SNAP-ON EMITTER

DRIP-EZE TAKE-APART

(Drawing by Michael Valdez)

saves valuable dollars, it saves water, and it is the only way to have a handsome garden without the chore of daily watering.

In areas where water is in short supply, a drip system is almost essential and if the water is saline (which is harmful to plants), drip systems are also called for. With regular watering, salty water can kill plants, but with drip watering, which adds small amounts slowly, the salinity is administered at a safe level.

Evaluate what types of plants you are growing before you select a drip system to install. Vegetable gardens will need water more often than an ornamental garden of shrubs and trees. Vegetables grow quickly and use up water quickly, as do flower gardens. A garden composed only of evergreens, however, can maintain itself on less water than the flower garden. Plan your garden first as to plants and then decide on the proper watering system for it.

Planning a System—Plan the drip system by sketching it on a piece of paper; use a sheet of graph paper sold at art stores and measure off the garden area in feet and inches. Now draw in the existing plants; use a different shape for shrubs, trees, flowers. It is not necessary to know landscape symbols—just draw in shapes for each plant so you have a plan or aerial-type drawing.

Which drip system should you choose? Should the pipe be above ground or below it? How should you lay it out—with spur line, in a channel pattern, or what? The answers to these questions depend on the type of garden and the topography of the land. But in almost every case there is a drip system to help you water your plants properly.

You can drip water to almost any plant, even grasses, although in the case of lawns the soaker drip system is used rather than the conventional emitter drip systems. You will need several drip setups for an entire garden area. Map out the site with existing plants as already suggested, and then sketch in systems as they would apply—a row pattern in one area perhaps (vegetables and flowers), or a point- or grid-system pattern in another place. The selection of the system depends on how many plants are in the garden and the distance between them.

Sometimes it is difficult to determine whether to use above- or below-ground installation. Most gardens have above-ground setups, but experts argue that below ground is where pipes should be. The answer lies in your own garden—if hoses and pipes on soil are conspicuous, then the more expensive underground system might be the answer. In many gardens, the placement of hoses on the soil does not seem to detract from the overall appearance because plants will cover the hoses.

How Much or How Often to Water—The area around the roots (the wet zone) is what is vital. You have to consider the size and the shape of the wet zone, which will vary according to the type of soil and the rate at which the emitters discharge water. Water moves downward and spreads in all directions by capillary action. In fine soil, the wet zone is circular in appearance whereas in coarse soil, which does not retain water long, the wet zone is elliptical.

Water should be applied slowly so it will be absorbed and not run off from application points. Runoff and puddling can be avoided by stopping the water and then turning it on again later. The time interval between one application of water and the next may range from 1 to 16 hours. If the time is more than 16 hours, you may have to increase the number of emitters.

To aid you in determining the amount of water certain groups of plants need—trees, shrubs, flowers—manufacturers generally include in their literature various watering charts. The charts are meant only as guidelines; watering needs will depend on plant type, sun and wind exposure, and soil composition. Climatic conditions vary throughout the United States; for example, in desert areas plants may require many more moisture applications than are described in supplier's charts. Your own experience with your garden will dictate changes in frequency, volume, and watering times.

The Garden—Let us start with a general plan—that is, flower borders and beds, with ornamental shrubs and trees as backgrounds. The main part of the garden is either a lawn or a patio. In this type of garden we opt for a perimeter system of hose, with spur lines and emitters coming off the main hose line, which is standard 1/4-inch hose. For a 20-by-30-foot garden the cost is minimal. Here, the line is set on top of the ground with emitters at specific places.

In a cutting garden we use a U-shaped layout for the drip system. Here the hoses are laid out in a conventional U, parallel to the rows of plants; this is an easy system to lay out and works well.

For the vegetable garden a U-shaped pattern again could be used, or a grid pattern of piping works well. Vegetables require a lot of water, so the spacing of the emitters is closer than in an ornamental garden.

Although the cost of the drip system for the vegetable garden may well be more than the cost of hoses or sprinklers or just about the same, the yield will be far greater than with conventional watering. You will have a bountiful harvest. If you are growing fruit trees, the drip system is a must—it will help to produce larger yields with very little work. Conventional watering systems for fruit trees leave a lot to be desired.

If you must watch your garden budget, the flower garden is the one place where you can install a small drip system and let nature (rain) do the rest. Even two drip system kits will supply moisture for the average flower garden; total cost is about $60. Drip watering eliminates most weeds, so the money spent is well worth it.

A drip system for a box or container garden requires a somewhat different installation because the lines must be run in the planter boxes themselves. For my deck garden, which is a box arrangement, the hose is secured to a wooden fence approximately 4 inches above the soil line of the wooden boxes. The slow trickle of water supplied continuously to the plants makes them grow rapidly. Before I installed the drip system, the soil was forever drying out because soil in boxes dries out much more quickly than ground soil. Ground plants can always reach out for moisture; roots confined to a box cannot.

My planter boxes are approximately 4 to 6 feet long, so installation was not difficult; however, if you have single boxes, there is a problem. You can still run a single emitter somewhere overhead if there is a suitable wooden post or other wooden member to which the hose or pipe can be attached. If there is not, then you must water by other methods.

CHAPTER THREE

How Plants Grow

Get acquainted with plants—know how they grow and what makes them grow—so you can care for them intelligently. It saves much unnecessary labor. A little knowledge about roots, stems, and leaves, and how they work together takes the mystery out of plants.

This chapter is not a technical treatise of plant growth. It explains in simple terms just what makes a plant grow and how it assimilates the elements to make its food. If you know what does what in a plant, you can become your own plant doctor and avoid panic if plants don't grow as they should. You will have some idea what is wrong with an ailing plant and how to take care of it.

Another part of successful gardening is knowing your climate. Knowledge of weather in your area can save you work and energy since climate dictates what you can and can't grow. Remember, working with nature makes gardening a pleasure; working against her is a chore.

BASIC PRINCIPLES OF PLANT GROWTH

Plant roots absorb water and other chemical substances that are necessary for plant growth. If roots don't get water, the plant dies.

The roots work in partnership with the leaves. Water absorbed by the roots and carbon dioxide taken in through pores in the leaves are the raw materials needed by the leaf *factory* to produce simple sugars using energy from the sun or other light sources—this manufacturing process is called photosynthesis. Chlorophyll (the green matter in plants) uses light energy to drive the process of photosynthesis.

The sugars made in the green leaves provide the building blocks for the plant's structures and the energy source for its life activities, including growth and reproduction.

BUYING PLANTS

It pays to buy the very best plants you can find because they are more likely to succeed. Hundreds of plants are available at nurseries and from mail-order suppliers. Seedling annuals and perennials are sold in flats or cartons (these are shallow wood or plastic containers). Your best buy is a flat of fifty or sixty plants. If you don't want to start your own plants from seed (which takes additional work and effort), seedlings in flats are a blessing. I sit on the small bench I made with the flat resting on an angled plywood board in my lap so I am at the height of the soil and can do my planting without backbreaking effort.

Shrubs and trees are sold balled and burlapped (B&B) or bare root. With the B&B method, a tree is dug from the ground with a ball of soil around it; it is then wrapped in burlap and tied at the crown with a string. Evergreen shrubs, conifers, and some deciduous shrubs are sold this way. (See Chapter 7 for more information.)

Plants sold in containers are available at nurseries during all the seasons and come in a variety of sizes and prices. If the plants are growing in metal cans, have the cans cut at the nursery to preserve the plant as well as your disposition.

Generally, nurseries will load your car for you, but since unloading at home is your job, don't buy anything that will be too heavy to carry. Flats and cartons of seedlings fit easily in your car trunk or back seat. (Ask your helper to protect your car from soil with paper liners.) Don't lift large trees and shrubs. Ideally you should have them delivered, but if you insist on carrying large plants in your car, make sure they don't obstruct your view.

Don't leave the newly purchased plants sitting in the garden in the sun; it weakens some and kills others (only a few don't mind). The shock of transplanting is enough for the plant to contend with in the beginning, so don't burden it unnecessarily. If plants are being delivered, make sure you or someone is there to receive them so they can be planted right away.

CLIMATE AND PLANTS

The advent of new gardening aids—fertilizers, insecticides, and other chemicals—has caused many people to lose sight of what gardening really is. Too often the homeowner sprinkles, sprays, feeds, and protects his plants in an endless program. But none of the new products are miracle workers; gardening is still working with nature, which includes climate.

Your area's climate has a tremendous influence on what kind of plants you can grow. Know how much rainfall your locale receives. (One of the blessings of arthritis is that you can forecast

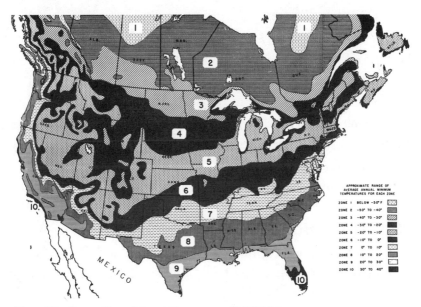

Plant Hardiness Zone Map (Courtesy of USDA)

23

your climate by how stiff your bones feel!) Sun, humidity, wind, and seasonal characteristics are also part of the gardening program. In every region, climatic factors are different—even in a 10-mile radius climate can vary considerably, especially if you are near hills, lakes, and streams. For example, my house is only 14 miles from San Francisco. In summer, the temperature is 15 degrees warmer here than it is in the city. Our annual rainfall is about 38 inches; in the city it is about 17 inches.

The East Coast has similar climatic differences within its own regions because of its varied topography. In the South, where moderate temperatures prevail all year, there is still another kind of gardening picture. Thus, a wise gardener, unlike the neophyte, will write for specific maps (available from the Weather Bureau) of his state.

Climate can be modified somewhat of course. You cannot stop the wind, but you can stop its harmful effects. Stop branches from breaking by having trees properly pruned. Grow fruit trees, which can be harmed by wind, in espalier fashion against walls and fences, and have hedges put in place to break the force of the wind.

If you are in a rainy area, be sure that sufficient drainage has been provided. The soil will be constantly leached, so be prepared to add fertilizer often. And in dry regions with scanty rainfall, remember that plants to some degree adapt to water shortage.

If there is too much sun, plant under trees or to the north of the building, but expect a reduction of flowering in plants. Provide a means of combating loss of moisture, which is the chief effect of excess sun (mulching the soil helps a great deal).

SOIL AND SOIL TESTING

Soil is the basis of practically all gardening. Although Japanese gardens may have only rocks and sand, most gardens have plants, trees, and shrubs. However, you can start to landscape only when the soil is properly prepared.

The soil in this terrace bed is poor and needs additives; you can determine the soil quality by looks—it is dry and grainy. (Photo by Ken Molino)

Earth or soil has two layers: topsoil and subsoil. The subsoil is beneath the surface layer; it has been there for hundreds of years, and it can be either a few inches or as much as twenty inches below the surface. The subsoil varies greatly in composition: it is sandy or claylike. A very sandy subsoil that retains little moisture is useless to plants. If it is composed of a great deal of clay, the subsoil holds water so long that plants literally drown. It should be broken up, or for severe cases, a drainage system should be installed.

A fertile topsoil, which is a mixture of clay, sand, and humus, is porous in texture and provides good drainage. Because it is spongy, the soil retains moisture. The humus provides good conditions for the growth of soil bacteria, which is essential for plant nutrition. This is the kind of soil we want in our garden, but in most cases it must be built by a program of soil conditioning.

A good porous soil has excellent water absorption, thus enabling moisture to be transported quickly through the pores to the roots of the plant. The pores also carry away excess water, thus preventing the topsoil from becoming soggy. Once soil is waterlogged, air can't circulate freely, and circulation is necessary for good plant growth.

Good drainage is essential for preventing a waterlogged situation that can kill plants. In such situations, plants develop shallow roots and perish from a lack of moisture since they can't reach down for the stored water. Poor drainage is a common fault of most soils and is generally caused by a layer of hard earth.

Improve the physical structure of the soil by turning it, keeping it porous, and using composts and mulches throughout the year. Porosity is the key to good soil; only when little air tubes are in the soil is it worthwhile to fertilize and work your garden. Fertilitizing alone won't provide for good plant growth; the physical condition or tilth of the soil is just as important in the overall working of the soil.

Dig up some soil on your property and crumble it in your hand. If it is lumpy and claylike, you must add sand and humus. If it is sandy and falls apart in your hand, you have to add some organic matter. A good soil crumbles between the fingers and feels like a well-done baked potato: porous with good texture.

HUMUS

Humus—animal manure, compost, leaf mold, and peat moss—is living organisms or their decayed remains. Humus adds body to light soils and provides aeration for claylike soils. Soil animals and micro-organisms break down humus, releasing its mineral elements so they can be used by growing plants. It is constantly decomposed and must be replaced, so maintenance of the proper proportion of humus in the soil is vital to good plant growth.

A convenient source of humus is peat moss, which is available at nurseries. There are differences between the various types of peat available, but through the years I have used many kinds and they all proved satisfactory. Leaf mold, another source of humus, is decayed leaves and grass clippings. Rake leaves into a pile and let them decompose. A third excellent source of humus is compost, which is basically decayed vegetable matter. (Composts are fully discussed in the next chapter.)

You must be your own judge about how much humus to add to soil. The amount depends on the soil, the kind of plants being grown, and the existing content of the humus. I mix about 1 inch of compost to about 6 inches of soil; this has proven satisfactory through the years for my garden.

Even though you add humus to the soil, you may also need to use fertilizers as a supplement. Fertilizers contain nitrogen, phosphorus, and potassium (potash). But fertilizers are not substitutes for humus, nor can decayed organic matter completely do the work of fertilizers—soil may need both.

pH SCALE

The pH scale is like a thermometer, but instead of measuring heat it measures the acidity or alkalinity of soil. Soil with a pH of 7 is neutral; below 7 the soil is acid, and above 7 it is alkaline.

It is important to know what kind of soil you have so that the

Getting a mulch pile together is fairly easy. (Photo by USDA)

maximum results of all fertilizers applied to it can be obtained. To determine the pH of your garden soil, have it tested by the state agricultural authorities or make your own test with one of the kits available from suppliers.

Most of our commonly grown trees and shrubs prefer a neutral soil; some grow better in an acid condition, and several types prefer an alkaline soil. But generally a soil reaction as nearly neutral as possible (between 6 and 7) allows you to grow the most plants successfully.

In alkaline soils potash becomes less and less effective and eventually becomes locked in. In very acid soils aluminum becomes so active that it becomes toxic to plants. Acidity in soil controls many functions: (1) it governs the availability of the food in the soil and determines which bacteria thrive in it, and (2) it somewhat affects the rate at which roots can take up moisture and leaves can manufacture food.

To lower the pH of soil (increase the acidity), apply ground sulfur at the rate of 1 pound to 100 square feet. (This lowers the pH of loam soil about one point.) Spread the sulfur on top of the soil and then apply water.

To raise (sweeten) the pH of soil, add ground limestone at the rate of 10 pounds per 150 square feet. Scatter the limestone on the soil, or mix it well with the top few inches of soil and water. It is better to add ground limestone or hydrated lime in several applications at 6- or 8-week intervals instead of using a lot at one time.

CHAPTER FOUR

How to Avoid Unnecessary Work

Working in the garden is good exercise for both the body and the mind. However, experience and time will teach you how to avoid doing unnecessary things so that your time can be utilized doing other, more interesting gardening (and in the end both the garden and you profit). For example, use mulches to protect plants and cut down on weeding, add good compost to your soil to avoid unnecessary spading and digging of old earth, and follow the proven ways of moving and handling large tubs and boxes.

MULCHES

A mulch is a covering of organic or inorganic material laid on exposed soil (generally around plants) in your garden. Grass clippings, leaf mold, shells, hulls of rice, peanut hulls, sawdust, or hay and straw are all organic mulches; that is, they decay in time and return to the soil. Inorganic mulches include newspapers, aluminum foil, and plastic sheeting.

Mulching does many things. It conserves moisture and also keeps the soil temperature cool in summer and warm in winter. Mulching discourages weeds and prevents a hard top crust from forming on soil. A mulch also protects plants from alternating freezing and thawing in winter, which can harm plants. And, above all, an organic mulch eventually decays and adds nutrients to your soil.

Types

There are many kinds of mulches, but the following seven are the most popular:

1. *Hay and straw*—These are inexpensive, deteriorate slowly, and are lightweight and easy to apply. (Salt hay is weed free, too.)

2. *Leaves*—Leaves make a good mulch, but remember to occasionally poke holes in the covering so air reaches the leaves or they can form a soggy wet covering. Oak leaves and pine needles are excellent for acid-loving plants such as rhododendrons and azaleas.

3. *Peat*—This widely used but expensive mulch smothers weeds effectively and holds water, but it can become an impervious mat that hinders water from reaching the soil.

4. *Cocoa beans and peanut shells*—Both these materials, when decomposed, add important nitrogen, phosphorus, and potash to the soil. They are easy to scatter, are not objectionable to look at, and are generally inexpensive.

5. *Tree bark*—This comes in many grades, but the medium-sized pellets are best. The bark decomposes slowly, is neat, and looks good in the garden. Once it was inexpensive but lately has increased tremendously in price.

6. *Sawdust*—Use it by itself or add it to other mulches.

7. *Inorganic mulches*—These do not add anything to the soil, but where they are available they can be used. Inorganic mulches include:

    (a) *Stones and pebbles*—Water passes through stones and pebbles, and plant roots are protected from temperature changes. They have the added bonus of being decorative.

    (b) *Polyethylene film*—This material—black or white—is difficult to set in place and eventually curls, so it is hardly attractive. If you use it, be sure to punch some holes in it so water can penetrate to the soil; otherwise, it may do more harm than good. Cover it with small pebbles or fir bark to keep it anchored to the ground. (A nice alternative to plastics is "Weed Barrier fabrics," which are air and water permeable but prevent weed growth.)

(c) *Newspapers*—Laid flat in place on the ground, newspapers make a better mulch than you may think. They may not look attractive, but they do the job.

(d) *Aluminum foil*—In my opinion this is much too expensive to use for mulching.

Mulches can be used advantageously on all plants except grasses and ground covers. Do not cover the crowns of the plants when spreading mulches; pile the material 2 to 3 inches thick up to the base of the plant. In California, we keep mulches in place all year, and I suggest this procedure for most parts of the country. However, if you can't keep the mulches in place all year, apply them after the soil has warmed up in spring and growth has started. If put on too early they may hinder growth somewhat because they tend to keep the soil cool. In fall, apply mulches after the soil has frozen.

COMPOSTS

A compost pile in most gardens seems undesirable, which is perhaps why they are seldom seen and why many gardeners have problems with soil and plants. Yet composting is a basic of successful gardening. Composting is making your own fertilizer and soil conditioner by using garden wastes such as twigs and leaves and kitchen wastes and whatever other organic material you don't want. The compost pile not only saves you money (you don't have to buy humus), it saves time and labor as well. A garden with composted soil is always a healthy garden, so you can lessen the chores of combating insects and tending unhealthy plants.

If you are squeamish about having the compost pile as part of the garden (because of odors), hide it near the garden—but close

Fresh topsoil has been added in this vegetable garden area; even a 2-inch layer will help stimulate old soil to grow. Work into old soil. (Photo by author)

enough so you can get to it. A small 5-by-5-foot bin can be constructed somewhere on the property to confine the compost or you can buy commercial metal compost units.

To build your own bins for composting, use 2-by-12-inch planks set inside 4-by-4-inch posts and fixed on three sides. Leave the fourth side open, or place a gate in it for easy access. Concrete blocks may also be used to fashion a bin.

To start the compost, add garden debris: raked leaves, twigs, and branches. Over this sprinkle some soil and then some manure. (Manure now comes in tidy packages at nurseries for the fastidious.) Build up layers, and sprinkle some lime on each layer (unless you garden in the western U.S.). Air is needed within the compost heap to keep organisms working, so from time to time punch holes into the heap with a broom handle. Be sure moisture gets to the heap too, but never saturate it. If you don't have enough rain, occasionally sprinkle the heap with water. After a few months, turn the heap, bringing the sides to the top. When you apply compost, put it on top of the soil and hoe it slightly; the idea is to leave the organic matter near the surface. Don't bury it.

Many types of soil conditioners and plant foods are at nursery suppliers. (Photo by author)

A more sophisticated method of making a compost heap involves putting materials through a shredder (available at garden suppliers); this speeds up the process considerably. You also might want to try chemicals that hasten the decaying process. They are available at nurseries under various trade names.

MOVING CONTAINERS

While moving recently, I had a large rhododendron (almost 8 feet tall) in a 28-inch tub. Since it was a favorite plant, I wanted to take it with me, but it weighed at least 600 pounds. To further add to my consternation, the plant was on a hillside about 12 feet up the slope. Even two strong backs (hired help) wouldn't be able to do the job. But an old Chinese gardener working across the street suggested the solution. He looked at the plant and muttered, "Slide it down on planks." I nodded and went about my business, but the next day I realized the validity of his idea. I had two boys who were working in my yard get two 2-by-12-inch redwood boards 12 feet long and prop them at the base of the container. The trick was to lift the box only once, just 2 or 3 inches, to get it on the boards. They did this in a few minutes, and I guided the planter and plant as it slid down the boards and rested in the yard. We were halfway home now.

The next step was to get the planter on a truck. I remembered the old burlap-bag method of pulling a plant. I put the bag on the pavement next to the plant. Once more the boys lifted the planter an inch or so onto the burlap; the rest was easy. We pulled the box across the yard to the truck. To get it on the truck we again propped the 2-by-12-inch boards against the truck floor and pushed the plant onto the truck.

Now when one of my fellow gardeners says I can't possibly move containers, I say "Think again." Most containers can be moved to another place on burlap and pulled across an area. Or you can ease boxes and tubs along on 2-inch steel poles. This is a slow procedure, but it works and saves back and leg work. Set two rollers under the box and start pushing the container along. Replace rollers as you continue the move. By the way, wooden dollies and casters for containers won't work in the garden unless you have pavement under them.

CHAPTER FIVE

No-bend Gardening:
Raised Planters

R aised planters (at waist level or higher) let you easily tend plants; for our school of gardeners this is reward enough—no more backaches and tedious bending! But there are other reasons for the popularity of elevated gardens: they allow for versatility when planning the garden; they relieve the monotony of a ground garden; and they put flowers and plants in a position that delights the eye.

Included in this chapter about raised planters are discussions about window boxes, step gardens, and shelf gardens. Thus, you'll discover old ways and new ways to enjoy your yard without straining the muscles. Raised planters give you the opportunity to work your garden and get enough (but not too much) exercise.

Making planters may seem complicated and beyond your capabilities, but simple planters can be built easily in an afternoon. Or, of course, you can have them made by a handyman or a carpenter.

PLANTERS AND BEDS

Because the planter or raised bed becomes part of the design of the garden, it should be planned carefully, with scale and balance kept in mind. Again, sketches on paper will help to decide just how many planters to arrange. A simple design is best because it can be used with almost any style of architecture while providing a good home for plants. We mention several kinds of planters in this chapter, but remember that you will have to design planters to your own specifications, which will vary depending on the site. A planter may be a window box or a raised unit that runs the entire length of the house, an arrangement of modular boxes, a step gar-

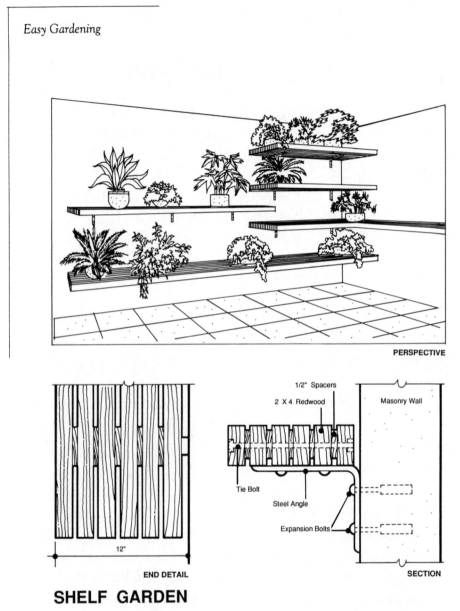

PERSPECTIVE

1/2" Spacers

2 X 4 Redwood

Masonry Wall

Tie Bolt

Steel Angle

Expansion Bolts

12"

END DETAIL

SECTION

SHELF GARDEN

(Drawing by Adrián Martínez)

den, and so forth. What you choose depends on the house and the site. In any case, the material for the planter should be impervious to the weather. Redwood or cypress is generally used because these materials do not need preservatives yet weather beautifully and last for years. Stone and concrete are other good materials.

An outdoor planter can be a freestanding or stationary type of any given design—triangular, oblong, or rectangular. Free-standing boxes create instant effects when used for patio borders or in corners; with geraniums and agapanthus, the patio becomes colorful in one afternoon. And portable units can be rearranged at any time—put them where you think they will look best.

Brick, stone, or slate stationary planters take time to make, but once built they are attractive, especially against a house wall. For footings a trench about 20 inches in depth must be dug, depending on the local frost line of the area.

WOODEN PLANTERS

Wood is a favorite material for raised planters and beds; it is easy to work with, and generally inexpensive in most areas; it is easily handled, hardly breaks or chips, and blends well in the garden. As mentioned, redwood and cypress tolerate weather and improve in appearance with age.

Because plant boxes come in many shapes, specific areas can be accommodated with boxes. The planters may be portable, or they can be affixed to become part of the garden design. Boxes can be stacked in tiers, arranged in grid fashion against the wall for easy gardening that eliminates stooping and squatting, or combined with longer or deeper planters to provide dimension and attractiveness, especially in small spaces. In fact, boxes are so versatile that there is no end to their uses for gardeners.

The thickness of the lumber you use depends on the box to be built; smaller boxes (up to 16-by-24 inches) can be made with 1-inch lumber. Larger boxes are best when made with 2-inch lumber. Use galvanized nails or brass screws when building planters. In the following pages we show many box-construction designs that you can apply to your garden.

Another variation of a plant box is the L-shaped container,

This brick planter puts plants up above ground level and makes tending the plants easier than if one had to bend. (Photo by author)

which combines wood and concrete to provide a gardening area against a house or garage corner. The back walls of these containers should be of brick or concrete to help ward off termites, and all wood should be kept at least 6 inches above soil line. You can also make divided and multilevel L-shaped containers, and there are dozens of ways to vary the arrangement to make it pleasing to the eye.

Terraced containers aren't difficult to make. They add great dimension to the garden, and if cleverly planned, with steps adjoining or dividing them, they are a blessing. Railroad ties are frequently used for this type of construction; the results are infinitely charming.

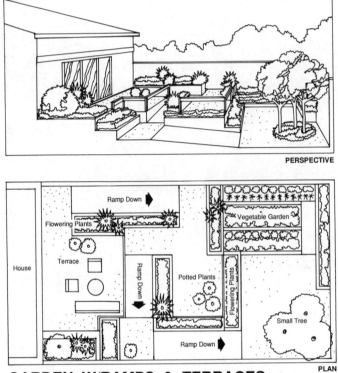

PERSPECTIVE

PLAN

GARDEN W/RAMPS & TERRACES
(Drawing by Michael Valdez)

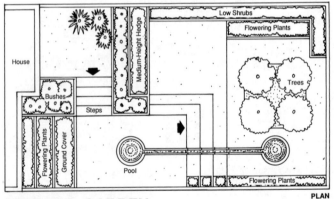

STEPPED GARDEN

(Drawing by Michael Valdez)

No matter how you decide to use plant boxes in your garden, you will find they take the ache out of gardening and contribute a great deal to an area. And don't think you can't make them yourself. Small boxes are well within the realm of our kind of gardening, and larger boxes—and these are useful too—can be made by a handyman or a carpenter. The initial cost may be high, but remember that these boxes will be with you for many years.

For Full Sun	For Partial Sun
Geranium	Browallia
Lantana	Heliotrope
Lobelia	Impatiens
Nasturtium	Begonia
Petunia	

For Partial Shade	Vines and Trailers
Aeschynanthus	Bougainvillea
Episcia	Cobaea scandens
Fuchsia	Thunbergia alata
Tuberous begonia	Tuberous begonias (pendula type)
Achimenes	

PREPARING PLANTER BEDS

Provide a porous soil for plants in masonry or wooden planters. Planters take money and time, especially if you have had them built, so it is senseless to have poor soil that will lead to ugly, dying plants.

Before you add fresh soil to a permanent planter, loosen the subsoil on which the box rests; do this with a small fork or hand cultivator. If soil is caked, water can't penetrate it, and all your work will be for nothing. Add some humus and compost and work it into the existing soil. Install a bed of crushed rock or gravel to

Planter beds at different levels allow gardeners with back trouble to have an easy time cultivating their plants. (Photo by Ken Molino)

facilitate drainage. Now add new soil to within 2 inches of the top of the planter, for easy watering.

Sun, hot air, and wind cause soil in planters to dry out rapidly, so if there isn't ample rainfall be sure to water plants copiously, especially during hot months. Water deeply and heavily. Keep weeds out of planters; once the planter is established and plants are growing well, weeds will seldom appear, but until then watch for stray weeds and remove them. Every other week during spring and summer add some plant food to the soil. Use a general fertilizer such as 10-10-5. (Granular form is the easiest; just sprinkle it on the soil and water.)

In winter, plants need protection from severe weather, so cover them with a thin mulch, or in the case of evergreens, be sure they get some attention.

PYRAMID GARDENS

Be daring with your no-bend gardens; a fine example is shown in the photograph of a pyramid design resplendent with succulents. This garden looks complicated, but it is simple to build, offers great beauty for little work, and the plants in it are very easy to care for. Planting pockets are wide enough to accommodate many kinds of plants, and the design of the planter provides shade and sun, so plants are not always in intense sun. Make shelves at least 10 to 12 inches deep and 7 to 8 inches wide for maximum use, and construct the planter from redwood.

This garden can be placed anywhere on the property for accent or may be used as the garden itself—fill planting pockets with rich soil and put plants in place. Our photograph shows succulents, but all kinds of plants can be used with equal success. The pyramid unit is ideal for annuals and perennials, vegetables, etc.

POLE-AND-POST: FLOATING GARDENS

Pole-and-post gardens may not strike you as real gardens when you first think of them. However, this no-bend kind of gardening really offers unlimited ways of growing plants in pots, and at waist and eye levels they make dramatic viewing. Commercial poles and containers are available from suppliers, but you can make your own designs with 4-by-4-inch posts that are either anchored into the ground with concrete or onto wood decks with L-shaped brackets.

The purpose of this garden in the air is not only to avoid bending when tending plants, but also to achieve dimension and drama. Bolt pots with holes in the bottom to posts and anchor the

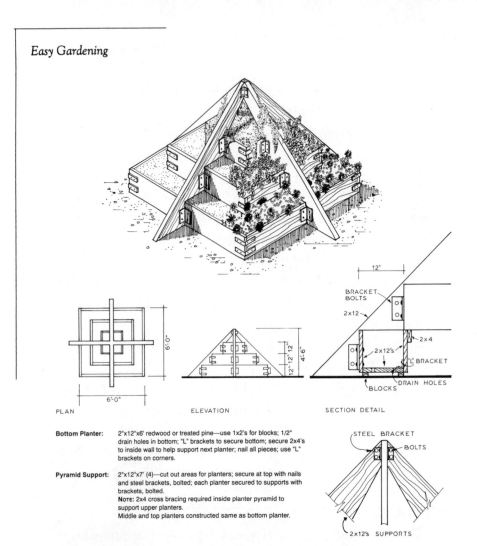

Bottom Planter: 2"x12"x6' redwood or treated pine—use 1x2's for blocks; 1/2" drain holes in bottom; "L" brackets to secure bottom; secure 2x4's to inside wall to help support next planter; nail all pieces; use "L" brackets on corners.

Pyramid Support: 2"x12"x7' (4)—cut out areas for planters; secure at top with nails and steel brackets, bolted; each planter secured to supports with brackets, bolted.
NOTE: 2x4 cross bracing required inside planter pyramid to support upper planters.
Middle and top planters constructed same as bottom planter.

Pyramid Garden
(Drawing by B. Holman)

posts in the ground (as mentioned above). The construction is so simple that in one afternoon you can have an attractive garden.

Place the containers—anything from clay pots to architectural bowls—one to a post, at varying heights to create constant interest. However, don't set them so high you can't easily reach the plants. If possible, use three or five in a group for a pleasing arrangement.

Try to use the same kind of container for each group. If you want, add pots to the post sides to create a tier garden, but avoid overloading the post. Simple pot hangers that clip onto the edge of standard clay pots are available for this arrangement.

You can grow almost anything, from annuals and perennials to vegetables and herbs, in this floating garden. (Trees and shrubs are of course beyond the post garden idea.) Use trailing plants and upright growers, and strive for an ideal arrangement. We grow ferns and trailers such as chlorophytum; they are stunning in such a situation, the entire plant can be seen, and they grow lavishly because foliage is never bruised. Cascading petunias and fuchsias are other stellar candidates for these unusual gardens, and don't forget upright plants such as asters.

Select an area with ample sun and some wind protection. You are creating a sculptural garden when you work with posts, so it is best to view this scene from a distance rather than close up.

This vine on an overhead trellis creates a beautiful garden entrance. (Photo by author)

TRELLIS AND ESPALIER GARDENING

There is a way to provide beauty and easy gardening with trellis gardening. In this case you garden vertically rather than employing the traditional horizontal gardening. To do trellis gardening, a support for plants is necessary; namely, trellises (sometimes called lattices). These structures of wood strips, usually 1 1/2 inches wide, are decorative as well as functional. Vegetables like squash and cucumbers can be grown on trellises, fruit trees can be espaliered on the supports for maximum growing, and climbing berries can do very well on trellises. Don't forget attractive vines, such as clematis and bougainvillea, that bring spring and summer color.

The advantages of a trellis garden are many, but perhaps the most important one is that you can grow plants easily without stooping and bending.

Trellis Gardening

Trellis gardening requires no more space than what a few planter boxes filled with soil need: an area about 8 feet long by 2 feet wide. By growing plants vertically you significantly increase growing space. Vertical gardening can be done on a back porch or in an entryway, and a verdant greenery can be created with trellises.

If your outdoor area is a patio, use some decorative arbors and trellises laced with plants to add charm to the garden. If the space is a doorway, grow some vegetables, or if somewhat larger, grow fruit trees against trellises. By extending the trellis work with an overhead canopy, you can create a beautiful hanging garden of vines (grapes, for example).

Trellises can also be used as fences, walls, screens, canopies, arbors, pergolas, and gazebos. There are numerous places to create your easy trellis garden.

If you are advancing into the middle years (or actually into the middle years), it is very good sense to garden intelligently; that is,

PATIO TRELLIS

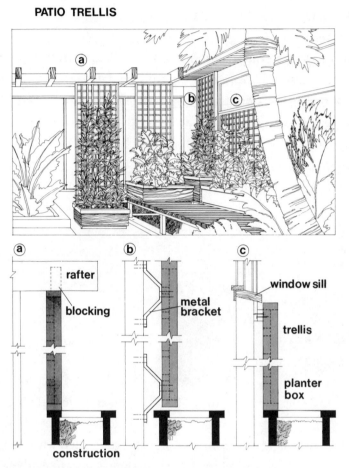

(Drawing by Michael Valdez)

without undue effort. Stooping and bending are fine exercises to a point, but too much is too much. It is much easier to walk around your garden and tend plants at waist and eye level than it is to have to lie or stoop on the ground. Also, you can see better in a standing position.

Trellis gardening thus affords you a less strenuous way to garden, and it also helps the plant. Air reaches all parts of the plant and when plants have a good circulation of air around them, they grow better. Also, growing plants vertically eliminates many insects simply because insects do not like to crawl any more than you do; horizontal fodder at ground level is a much easier dinner for some insects.

If you look at old neighborhoods, weatherworn trellises from years ago still stand. You can make trellises with very little carpentry knowledge, and once trellises are constructed, their installation is simple. You can secure them to the ground with posts or with stakes. The trellis can be built against a fence or wall, utilizing otherwise useless space, or it can be nailed to the planter box or staked in soil, depending on the situation. A homemade trellis is also inexpensive.

Even a simple trellis (at left) will add old world charm to a garden. (Photo by author)

At the start, adapting plants like vegetables and vines to trellises requires some work because plants have to be tied and trained. However, once started and tied by the stems at the bottom of the wood support, plants grow easily on a vertical course. Many plants have grasping tendrils or discs—and grow luxuriantly. They need occasional training; try tying the stems with string or plastic tie-ons (available at suppliers) to the wood members.

Besides the utilitarian features of trellises, they are charming in a garden. The wood structure provides vertical eye interest in otherwise horizontal stretches of garden; this is good garden design, balancing the horizontal and vertical lines.

An inexpensive, homemade, well-built trellis is quite versatile, but it must be used correctly. In many cases it is not wise to use too many plants—a tangle of foliage and stem may result. Here are six general suggestions when using trellises:

1. For smaller plants with small leaves, closer trellising is necessary.
2. When spanning a distance, trellises should always be in sections, with posts at intervals, to supply needed vertical accent when one design is repeated for a long distance without a break.
3. Laths must always be arranged to give adequate support for plants (where used exclusively for plants); laths must be close enough to permit small shoots to be secured.
4. If you are training plants against a flat surface (espalier), use a trellis pattern that has sufficient space between slats, generally 4 to 6 inches. Although many patterns are available, the grid pattern works best for espaliers.
5. Where shade and seclusion is paramount, use a close-patterned trellis to create a visually dramatic look in the intimate nook.
6. If there is a valuable scene on the other side of the trellis,

space strips far apart so the peek-through look is achieved. This is quite handsome.

Espalier

Espaliering, or training plants to a flat surface and to specific patterns, is not new, but it is certainly an overlooked part of gardening. A well-grown espalier against a trellis can be very attractive.

Espaliering is working against a flat surface. A plant grown in espalier style needs training and trimming to a desired shape. Generally, the plant is tied to a trellis that is parallel to a flat surface, with 4 to 6 inches of air space behind the plant. (In some cases, espaliers are applied directly to a wall.)

Many people want to grow delicious fruits, but may not have space for the plants. Espalier the trees on trellises and have all the fruit you want. For example, in a space of 20 feet, say against a fence, you can grow four dwarf fruit trees.

To break up a blank wall or fence use a small espalier; most plants adapt easily to this kind of growing. (Photo by author)

Buy (at a nursery) an espalier already started; they come in 5 gallon containers. It is much easier to train a tree or shrub that is already started than to initiate the pattern yourself. Don't rush espaliers; they take time to grow and cover an area, but once established, they are indeed handsome.

Years ago there were rigid espalier patterns, but now the designs are personal choices. The formal patterns, although still seen, are not as popular as the informal or free-form espaliers. The formal patterns are quite symmetrical and include the following:

- *The double horizontal cordon.* A center shoot about 20 inches high, with two horizontal branches in each direction.
- *The vertical U shape.* A vertical stem on each side of a central trunk. Double and triple U shapes are also seen.
- *The palmette verrier.* A handsome candelabra pattern.
- *The palmette oblique.* Branches trained in a fan shape.
- *The horizontal T.* A multiple horizontal cordon with several horizontals on each side of a vertical trunk.
- *Belgian espalier.* A diamond pattern.
- *Arcure.* A series of connecting arcs.

Informal espaliers are more natural and are casual or free-form. The informal espalier does not require religious trimming and training as does the formal pattern, but creating an open and beautiful design is still the goal. Supports are generally not necessary; you can tie stems of plants to surfaces with special nails or copper wire.

Espalier fruit trees can be grown in containers or in the ground. Use a well-drained, rich soil, and choose appropriate plants for the conditions you can give them. For example, put sun lovers against a south wall and shade lovers in a north or west exposure.

Fruit Trees

Fruit trees bear at different times of the year. For example, there are apples for early season, midseason, and late season (well into fall), so it is wise to select trees for the season you want. Just how long it will be before trees will bear is another consideration; apples and pears bear in 4 to 6 years; plums, cherries, and peaches bear in about 4 years.

Besides considering bearing season and length of bearing, you should also think of size. In addition to standard-sized fruit trees there are dwarf varieties that grow only a few feet. There are also different kinds of apples, peaches, or cherries; your local nursery will tell you about these. Your nursery also stocks the type of trees that do best in your area, so ask for advice. Your trees must be hardy enough to stand the coldest winter and the hottest summer in your vicinity.

Many varieties of fruit trees are self-sterile, which means that they will not set a crop unless other blossoming trees are nearby to furnish pollen. Some fruit trees are self-pollinating or fruiting and need no other tree. When you buy your fruit trees, ask about this. Fruit trees are beautiful just as decoration, but you also want fruits to eat.

Buy from local nurseries if possible, and look for 1- or 2-year-old trees. Stone fruits are usually 1 year old and apples and pears are generally about 2 years old at purchase time. Select stocky and branching trees rather than spindly and compact ones because espaliering requires a well-balanced tree.

Whether you buy from a local nursery or from a mail-order source (and this is fine too), try to get the trees into the ground as quickly as possible. Leaving a young fruit tree lying around in hot

To save on space espalier trees against a wall or fence; the effect is eye pleasing. (Photo courtesy of Western Wood Products)

sun can kill it. If for some reason you must delay the planting time, heel in the tree. This is temporary planting: dig a shallow trench wide enough to receive the roots, set the plants on their sides, cover the roots with soil, and water them. Try to keep new trees out of blazing sun and high winds.

Prepare the ground for the fruit trees with great care. Do not just dig a hole and put the tree in. Fruit trees do require some extra attention to get them going. Work the soil a few weeks before planting. Turn it over and poke it. You want a friable workable soil with air in it, a porous soil. Dry sandy soil and hard clay soil simply will not do for fruit trees, so add organic matter to existing soil. This organic matter can be compost (bought in tidy sacks) or other humus.

Plant trees about 10 to 15 feet apart in fall or spring when the land is warm. Then hope for good spring showers and sun to get the plants going. Dig deep holes for new fruit trees, deep enough to let you set the plant in place as deep as it stood in the nursery. (Make sure you are planting trees in areas that get sun.) Make the diameter of the hole wide enough to hold the roots without crowding. When you dig the hole, put the surface soil to one side and the subsoil on the other so that the richer top soil can be put back directly on the roots when you fill in the hole. Pack the soil in place firmly but not tightly. Water plants thoroughly but do not feed. Instead, give the tree an application of vitamin B12 (available at nurseries) to help it recover from transplanting.

Place the trunk of the fruit tree about 12 to 18 inches from the base of the trellis; you need some soil space between the tree and the wood. Trellises may be against a fence or dividers or on a wall. Young trees need just a sparse pruning. Tie branches to the trellis with tie-ons or nylon string, not too tightly but firmly enough to keep the branch flat against the wood. As the tree grows, do more trimming and tying to establish the espalier pattern you want.

To attach the trellis to a wall use wire or some of the many gadgets available at nurseries specifically for this purpose. For a masonry wall, rawl plugs may be placed in the mortared joints, and screw eyes inserted. You will need a carbide drill to make holes in masonry.

Caring for fruit trees is not difficult. Like all plants, fruit trees need a good soil (already prepared), water, sun, and some protection against insects. When trees are actively growing, start feeding with fruit tree fertilizer (available at nurseries). Use a weak solution; it is always best to give too little rather than too much because excess fertilizer can harm trees.

Observe trees frequently when they are first in the ground because this is the time when trouble, if it starts, will start. If you see leaves that are yellow or wilted, something is awry. Yellow leaves indicate that the soil may not contain enough nutrients. The soil could lack iron, so add some iron chelate to it. Wilted leaves could mean that water is not reaching the roots or insects are at work.

CHAPTER SIX

Special Gardens

I f the rigors of full-time gardening are beyond your capacity there are other kinds of special gardens to give you a chance to work with the soil and enjoy flowers. Growing plants in containers is one way; plants in stone or concrete trays is another way. And, too, there are special gardens for people with special needs. Gardening is really for everyone! It is just a question of the kind of garden that suits your needs and capacity.

CONTAINER GARDENS

Plants in pots or ornamental containers are always decorative and scores of people use them. Container gardens are also well suited to people with minor handicaps, for they offer a way to garden without too much work. The arrangement of the garden is up to you, and if one plant doesn't work, it is easy to move it to another place until a satisfying scheme is achieved.

Small or large containers—wood or clay—can be used depending on just what you want. They may be grouped together, or you can have modular wooden planters in different arrangements. The container garden can be an ever-changing landscape—using seasonal plants through spring, summer, and fall.

Almost any plant can be grown in containers: annuals, perennials, bulbs, small trees, and shrubs. Even vegetables can be grown in containers if that is your preference. The main thing is to arrange the containers in pleasing groups rather than just an isolated pot here or there. And do seek ornamental tubs and jardinieres to make the garden unique.

In winter, move plants indoors to enjoy them on gray days.

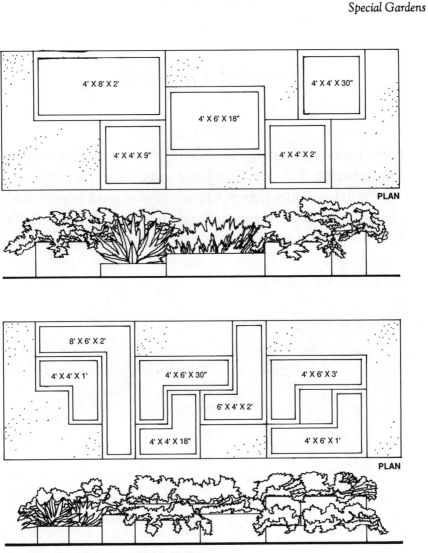

MODULAR PLANTERS

(Drawing by Michael Valdez)

Come spring put them outside to decorate your patio or garden. Maintenance, after initial planting, is simple: frequent waterings and light feeding of plants. Don't forget that flowering plants such as annuals and perennials will need much sun.

Remember that container gardening makes it possible for you

A small island garden such as this is easy to care for—just a watering in the morning now and then.(Photo by author)

to do as much or as little as you please, and the garden can be as small or as large as you think you can manage. A small vegetable garden keeps work to a minimum and provides a maximum harvest.

WHEELCHAIR GARDENS

A garden with properly planned paths can be used by wheel-

This is an easy garden to care for if one is not too enthusiastic about gardening— just a few plants and a bamboo as accent. (Photo by Tom)

chair gardeners, but make the paths wide and smooth for easy locomotion. Plywood boards are suitable for the paths and can be easily installed by a handyman. Remember that beds and borders can't be too wide because for easy cultivation you must have access from both sides.

Don't make the garden too large, but do plant it so it is attractive. Of course, the garden will have to be dug and planted, but once it is established wheelchair gardeners can find considerable work to keep them active in all seasons but winter. There will be enough to do, but not so much that gardening becomes tiresome.

A garden in the woodlands may seem like a great deal of work but it is not—bulbs multiply quickly and bloom year after year with little care. (Photo by Molly Adams)

Incorporate as many raised beds as possible (see Chapter 5) for easy gardening, and use container plants as accents. You can even grow small trees in suitable containers for garden decoration.

Use modern tools to work the garden; an invaluable tool is a light push-pull type of hoe with a long handle. Other similarly designed tools are also available from suppliers, or make your own.

STONE AND TRAY GARDENS

I see more and more of this type of gardening. Miniature gardens in sinks, troughs, etc., offer a wonderful outlet for people who want to exercise their creative sense and keep their fingers and mind busy. The sink garden is a fine place to grow alpines and rock garden plants, and flowers more charming than these are difficult to find. They are not easy to grow, but the bounty of bloom is well worth the challenge.

Concrete sinks and troughs are hard to find but concrete birdbaths and stone containers are available, and if they are 4 to 6 inches deep, they can be used. Even terra cotta drip saucers (now available in large sizes and depths) can be sink gardens, or you can make your own concrete containers. Whatever you use, be sure it has plenty of drainage holes in the bottom and is strong, weather resistant, and deep enough to hold small trees or shrubs.

The big advantage of sink gardening is that at waist level it eliminates stooping and squatting. And, too, the garden is elevated and easy to see and can be placed almost anywhere on the property, although a protected place with half sun is preferred. Use bricks, concrete blocks, or pedestal posts to support the miniature landscape.

Start the sink garden by covering the bottom of the container with about a half inch of small stones. Then add a thin layer of moist peat moss. Now add soil to about one-third the depth of the container. Press the soil in place to eliminate air pockets, and shape the soil in attractive hills and valleys for eye interest. Do not immediately plant—first move the potted plants around in the garden until you find the right place for them. Then remove them from their pots with as much root ball intact as possible and plant. Add gravel paths, small stones, and other decorations to make the setting handsome.

A sink garden is heavy when filled with soil and plants, so remember to assemble it in a permanent place. These gardens are essentially for the outdoors, but some can be grown in an unheated but not freezing room where there is ample light. Most outdoor gardens will need some protection from winter weather. Cover them with oak leaves, hay, or straw, as you would mulch a regular garden.

Watering depends on the weather and the kind of plants being grown as well as the soil mix and size of the garden. Buy plants from mail-order suppliers who specialize in rock garden and alpine species.

CUT FLOWER GARDENS

Your own cutting garden will give you hours and days of pleasure with your very own flowers. But it just will not do to cut the flowers and dump them into a vase of water. You must know how to cut flowers, how to prepare them for arrangements, and how to keep them living as long as possible.

It is wise to remember that a cut flower is still a living thing and, although taken from its mother plant, still needs nourishment and care. So let us see how to cut flowers, arrange them, and keep them indoors as long as possible.

At first you may think that a section on how to cut flowers is superfluous; but it is not, because flowers cannot be ripped from plants haphazardly nor can they be picked at any time. There is a time to cut flowers, just as there is a time to plant them. And different flowers require different handling techniques because plants have different types of stems: hairy, woody, hollow, and so on.

The main point to remember when cutting flowers is that, once cut, they still require water, and as quickly as possible. You can, if you have time, carry a jug of tepid water with you and plunge the flowers, after cutting, into the water, but this is usually a chore. Just cut and carry and get the flowers into the kitchen and into warm water as soon as possible. If you cut flowers and then leave them for even 30 minutes out of water, you are doing them an injustice.

It is best to avoid cutting flowers in the heat of the day (the old wives' tale about morning cutting is quite valid); cut the flowers in early morning or at dusk. In the early morning and evening the plants' stems are filled with water and in better condition to survive cutting.

As you go to cut flowers, carry with you a suitable basket or container to put the flowers in; it is messy to try and cut flowers with one hand and hold them in the other. Be sure you have sharp knives or scissors because you want to make clean cuts, never ripping gashes. If you crush the capillary vessels in the stems, they cannot take up water later. Sterilize cutters occasionally to help prevent spreading bacteria to the flower stem and plant. I sterilize my cutters simply by running a match flame over them. You may prefer to be more professional and dunk them in a sterilizing solution, which is fine.

When you cut flowers, select those that are almost open; the buds should show flower color. Some asters, chrysanthemums, and zinnias can be cut more fully open than other flowers but, generally, cut when the bud is partially open and color is showing.

Always cut stems at a slant, for a simple reason: this exposes more of the stem surface to water. And always cut the stem below a node; cutting at midpoint can weaken the plant. Handle flowers gingerly; do not smash them around or treat them like a sack of potatoes. True, they can take some mishandling, but why stretch your luck? Flowers are fragile when cut, so handle them carefully.

When you get flowers cut and in water, soak them to their necks at room temperature for about 2 hours. Then move the flowers and container to an airy, cool (65°F.) place, overnight if possible. In a cool spot at night, plants transpire little; thus, stems and leaves stay crisp and filled with water.

When you are ready to arrange your flowers, recut the stems. Plants with woody stems should be split (from the bottom, 6 to 8 inches), and you can smash these stems with a tap of a hammer. Immerse hairy-stemmed plants in tepid water. Recut hollow-stemmed flowers under water. (Plants with oozy stems should be seared with a match flame.)

Recutting stems under water may sound silly, but it does help preserve the quality of flowers like snapdragons, China asters, marguerites, sweet peas, and marigolds. What happens is that air bubbles can form during the brief period it takes to cut the flowers. The bubbles form because the crushed stems cannot take up moisture. If you slice off 1/4 inch of the stem under water, it prevents a new air bubble from forming.

When flowers are arranged, strip all leaves below the water line because foliage decomposes rapidly. Most flowers are not fussy about the quality of water, so regular tap water is fine. A few chips of charcoal will keep water sweet and odorless.

There are packaged, prepared chemicals that come with cut flowers from florist shops; use them if you like. Quite frankly, I have never seen any difference between flowers in plain water or flowers with chemicals added to the water—the flowers in either instance last the same time.

Hints for Cutting Specific Flowers

Through the years I have found that different flowers respond to different treatment; here is a rundown on how to cut and handle some favorite flowers.

Aster	Cut flowers when they are nearly open. Then place them in warm water. Recut stems under water. Lasts about 3 weeks.
Baby's Breath	Cut sprays when they are nearly half-open. Condition flowers in cold water overnight. Lasts 2 weeks.
Bachelor's Button	Cut flowers when they are three-fourths open. Split stems in warm water. Condition overnight. Lasts 2 weeks.
Calendula	Cut flowers when they are almost open. Condition overnight. Lasts 2 weeks.
Calla Lily	Cut at any stage. Submerge in cold water for a few hours and then remove. Cut stems

again under water. Lasts 2 weeks.

Candytuft	Cut when flowers are half-open. Condition in cold water overnight. Lasts 2 weeks.
Carnation	Cut when flowers are almost open. Recut stems at a slant under water. Let stand in cold water for one hour or so before arranging in tepid water. Lasts over 2 weeks.
Chrysanthemum	Cut when flowers are almost open. Place in warm water. Crush woody stem varieties, and condition overnight. Can be recut after about 14 days and revitalized in warm water. Lasts 2 weeks.
Clarkia	Cut flowers when they are almost open. Crush stems, and condition in cold water overnight. Lasts 10 days.
Dahlia	Cut flowers when they are fully open. Condition overnight in cool water. Lasts 10 days.
Delphinium	Cut when half of the flower spike shows color. Condition overnight in cool water. Lasts about 10 days.
Dianthus	Cut when flowers are half-open. Crush stems. Condition overnight in cool water. Lasts about 1 week.
Forget-Me-Not	Cut when flowers are half-open. Condition in warm water overnight. Recut and replace in warm water next day. Lasts 5 days.
Gerbera	Cut flowers when they are open. Condition in cold water overnight. Lasts about 1 week.
Larkspur	Cut when spray is about one-fourth open. Place stems in water and condition overnight. Flowers last about 1 week.

Marguerite	Cut flowers when they are fully open. Recut stems under cold water. Lasts 10 days.
Marigold	Cut flowers when they are open. Recut stems and then place in cold water. Lasts about 14 days.
Rose	Cut when three-quarters open. Cut stems so that two leaf nodes remain on plant; cut just above this second node or eye. Cut in late afternoon. Recut stem under a leaf node and split; then remove foliage from base of stem. Condition in cold water overnight if possible. Lasts about 1 week.
Snapdragon	Cut when flowers are half-open and condition in tepid water overnight. Lasts several days.
Stock	Cut when flowers are almost fully open. Condition in cold water overnight if possible. Lasts about 10 days.
Tulip	Cut when in full bud; make cut above white portion on the stem. Put stems in deep water up to buds. In 4 to 6 days recut stems, submerge again, and use. Lasts about 1 week.
Wallflower	Cut when nearly open. Soak stems in cold water. Lasts about 1 week.
Zinnia	Cut when flowers are almost completely open. Remove almost all leaves. Submerge in cold water for a few hours. Lasts about 10 days.

Keeping Flowers Fresh

Many times, after people cut flowers and put them in a vase of water, they forget them. Do not do this. Cut flowers, like any living plant, absorb water, and water evaporates. Thus, in one short sentence: Replenish water daily, and your flowers will last a long time. After several days, you might want to recut stems to a shorter length and rearrange flowers; this will prolong the flowers' lives by several days. Finally, you can use the flowers one last time in another variation by floating them in water.

To keep flowers fresh, keep them out of drafts; they last significantly longer in a quiet place. If night temperatures are cool, flowers will last longer than in a heated room. Also, it is best to keep flowers away from direct sunlight, which can wilt them.

CHAPTER SEVEN

Stocking the Garden

T he garden will glow if you plant vibrantly colored annuals and perennials. Although there may be difficult kinds, there are an equal number of easy ones that require only sowing to put the garden in a festive mood. Trees and shrubs, the backbone of a good garden, can be easily installed too. But remember that planting time—spring or fall—is as important as selection. Fortunately, however, even if you go wrong in selecting the right season for planting, most trees and shrubs will survive provided they are suitable for your climate zone.

ANNUALS AND PERENNIALS

Annuals produce flowers, mature, and then die in one season. They can be either grown from seed or purchased cheaply at the correct season and merely set into the ground with little trouble. However, with this latter method you must bend, whereas with seeds you merely stand and scatter. Most annuals are prolific bloomers that require little more than sun and water, but don't forget that annuals flower only once, so you'll need other plants if you want continuous color.

A perennial is a plant that generally blooms the second year after it is planted and thrives for many seasons. Thus, if you plant perennials you'll have color for several years. Buy seedlings at nurseries or grow your own from seed.

Be sure to put both annuals and perennials where they will receive plenty of sun or bloom will be sparse. Water them frequently and profusely because these plants need good moisture to really thrive. Following is a list of some of the most popular annuals and perennials.

ANNUALS

Botanical and Common Name	Approx. Height, Inches	Range of Colors	Peak Blooming Season	Sun or Shade
Antirrhinum majus (common snapdragon)	10 to 48 PD* 10 to 18	Large choice of color and flower form	Late spring and fall; summer where cool	Sun
Arctotis stoechadifolia grandis (blue-eyed African daisy)	16 to 24 PD 10	Yellow, rust, pink, white	Early spring	Sun
Begonia x semperflorens (wax begonia)	6 to 18 PD 6 to 8	White, pink, deep-rose, single or double flowers	All summer; perennial in temperate climate	Sun or shade
Calendula officinalis (calendula or pot marigold)	12 to 24 PD 12 to 15	Cream, yellow, orange, apricot	Winter where mild; late spring elsewhere	Sun
Centaurea cyanus (bachelors button or corn flower)	12 to 30 PD 12	Blue, pink, wine, white	Spring where mild; summer elsewhere	Sun
Clarkia amoena (godetia or farewell-to-spring)	18 to 30 PD 9	Mostly mixed colors white, pink, salmon, lavender	Late spring; summer where cool	Sun or shade

*PD = planting distance in inches

71

Plant	Height / PD	Color	Season	Exposure
Coreopsis tinctoria (calliopsis)	8 to 30 PD 18 to 24	Yellow, orange, maroon, and splashed bicolors	Late spring to summer; late summer where cool	Sun
Delphinium ajacis (rocket larkspur)	18 to 60 PD 9	Blue, pink, lavender, rose, salmon, carmine	Late spring to early summer	Sun
Dianthus species (pinks)	6 to 30 PD 4 to 6	Mostly bicolors of white, pink, lavender, purple	Spring and fall; winters where mild	Sun
Eschscholzia californica (California poppy)	12 to 24 PD 9	Gold, yellow, orange; "Mission Bell" varieties include pink and rose	Winter and spring in mild climates	Sun
Gaillardia pulchella (rose-ring Gaillardia)	12 to 24 PD 9	Zoned patterns in warm shades; wine, maroon	All summer	Sun
Godetia amoena (See *Clarkia amoena*)				
Gypsophila elegans (baby's breath)	12 to 30 PD 6	White, rose, pink	Early summer to fall but of short duration	Sun
Helianthus annuus (common garden sunflower)	36 to 120 or more PD 3	Yellow, orange, mahogany, or yellow with black centers	Summer	Sun

Plant	Height / PD	Colors	Season	Light
Helichrysum bracteatum (strawflower)	24 to 48 PD 9 to 12	Mixed warm shades; yellow, bronze, orange, pink, white	Late summer, fall	Sun
Impatiens balsamina (garden balsam)	8 to 30 PD 9	White, pink, rose, red	Summer to fall	Light shade; sun where cool
Lathyrus odoratus (sweet pea, winter-flowering)	36 to 72 PD 6	Mixed or separate colors, all except yellow, orange, and green	Late winter where mild	Sun
Lobelia erinus (edging lobelia)	2 to 6 PD 6 to 8	Blue, violet, pink, white	Summer	Sun, light shade
Lobularia maritima (sweet alyssum)	4 to 12 PD 12	White, purple, lavender, rosy-pink	Year-round where mild; spring to fall elsewhere	Sun, light shade
Matthiola incana (stock)	12 to 36 PD 9 to 12	White, cream, yellow, pink, rose, crimson-red, purple	Winter where mild; late spring elsewhere	Sun
Mirabilis jalapa (four-o-clock)	36 to 48 PD 12	Red, yellow, pink, white; some with markings	All summer	Light shade or full sun

Plant	Height / PD	Colors	Bloom time	Exposure
Petunia hybrids	12 to 24 PD 6 to 12	All colors except true blue, yellow, and orange	Summer and fall	Sun
Phlox drummondii (annual phlox)	6 to 18 PD 6 to 9	Numerous bicolors; all shades except blue and gold	Late spring to fall	Sun, light shade
Salpiglossis sinuata (painted tongue)	18 to 36 PD 9	Bizarre patterns of red, orange, yellow, pink, and purple	Early summer	Sun, light shade
Tagetes erecta (hybrids and species) (big or African marigold)	10 to 48 PD 12 to 18	Mostly yellow, tangerine, and gold	Generally, all summer	Sun
T. patula (hybrids and species) (French marigold)	6 to 18 PD 9	Same as African types, also russet, mahogany, and bicolors	Early summer	Sun
T. tenuifolia signata (signet marigold)	10 to 24 PD 9 to 12	Small; yellow, orange	Generally, all summer	Sun
Zinnia angustifolia (Mexican zinnia)	12 to 18 PD 6 to 9	Yellow, orange, white, maroon, mahogany	Summer	Sun
Z. elegans (small-flowered zinnia)	8 to 36 PD 9	Red, orange, yellow, purple, lavender, pink	Summer	Sun
Z. elegans (giant-flowered zinnia)	12 to 36 PD 12	Same colors as small-flowered zinnia	Summer	Sun

*PD = planting distance in inches.

PERENNIALS

Botanical and Common Name	Approx. Height, Inches	Range of Colors	Peak Blooming Season	Sun or Shade
Althea rosea (Alcea rosea) (hollyhock)	60 to 108	Most colors except true blue and green	Summer	Sun
Alyssum saxatile (Aurinia saxatilis) (basket of gold)	8 to 12	Golden-yellow, tinged with chartreuse	Early spring	Sun
Anemone coronaria (poppy-flowered anemone)	to 18	Red, blue, white	Spring	Sun
Asclepias tuberosa (butterfly weed)	24 to 36	Orange	Summer	Sun
Aster, dwarf type	8 to 15	Red, blue, purple	Late summer	Sun
Campanula carpatica (tussock bellflower)	8 to 10	Blue, white	Summer	Sun
C. persicifolia (willow bellflower)	24 to 36	White, blue, pink	Summer	Sun
Chrysanthemum coccineum (pyrethrum or painted daisy)	24 to 36	White, pink, red	Early summer	Sun

Plant	Height	Color	Bloom time	Light
C. maximum (daisy chrysanthemum)	24 to 48	White	Summer, fall	Sun or shade
C. x morifolium (florist's chrysanthemum)	18 to 30	Most colors except blue	Late summer, fall	Sun
Convallaria majalis (lily-of-the-valley)	9 to 12	White, pink	Spring, early summer	Light to medium shade
Coreopsis grandiflora	24 to 36	Golden yellow	Summer	Sun
Delphinium hybrid (Connecticut Yankee)	24 to 36	Blue, violet, white	Early summer	Sun
Dianthus barbatus (sweet William)	10 to 30	White, pink, red; zoned and edged	Early summer	Sun or light shade
Felicia amelloides (blue daisy)	20 to 24	Blue	Spring, summer	Sun
Gaillardia x grandiflora (blanket flower)	24 to 48	Yellow or bicolor	Summer, fall	Sun
Gazania hybrids	10 to 12	Yellow and brown bicolors	Summer, fall; spring where mild	Sun
Gypsophila paniculata (baby's breath)	24 to 36	White	Early summer and summer	Sun
Helenium (various) (sneezeweed)	24 to 48	Orange, yellow, rusty shades	Summer, fall	Sun

Plant	Height	Color	Bloom time	Light
Hemerocallis (various) (day lily)	12 to 72	Most colors except blue, green, violet	Midsummer	Sun or light shade
Hosta plantaginea (fragrant plantain lilly)	24 to 30	White flowers, yellow-green leaves	Late summer	Light shade
Iris (various) (bearded iris)	3 to 10 (dwarf); 15 to 28 (intermediate); 24 to 48 (tall)	Many, many colors	Spring, early summer	Sun or light shade
Iris cristata (crested iris)	6 to 8	Lavender, light blue	Spring	Light shade
Kniphofia (various) (torch lily)	24 to 72	Cream, white, yellow, orange	Early summer	Sun
Liatris pycnostachya (gayfeather)	60 to 72	Rose-purple	Summer	Sun or light shade
Lobelia cardinalis (cardinal flower or Indian pink)	24 to 36	Red	Late summer	Sun or light shade
Rudbeckia hirta (black-eyed Susan)	36 to 48	Yellow, pink, orange, white	Summer	Sun or light shade
Salvia patens (blue salvia sage or gentian sage)	24 to 36	Dark blue	Summer, fall	Sun

Plant	Height	Color	Bloom	Exposure
Scabiosa caucasica (pincushion flower)	24 to 30	White, blue, purple	Summer, fall	Sun
Solidago (various) (goldenrod)	20 to 36	Yellow	Summer	Sun or light shade
Veronica (various) (speedwell)	24 to 36	Blue, pink, white	Midsummer	Light shade
Viola cornuta (horned viper)	6 to 8	Purple; newer varieties in many colors	Spring, fall	Light shade
Yucca filamentosa (Adam's needle)	36 to 72	White	Late summer	Sun

Annuals, perennials, vines—it all adds up to a handsome garden and an easy-to-care-for one. (Photo by Matthew Barr)

TREES

Trees are a necessary part of any attractive garden, so don't be hesitant about using some (but not so many that the garden becomes a totally shaded place where nothing else will grow). And don't be afraid to plant seedlings because you think they won't grow while you're alive—like children, trees grow before you know it. Furthermore, there *are* fast-growing trees and smaller trees that mature more quickly. There are trees for all situations, and your local nursery can help you select trees for your area, but first know something about trees so you can talk intelligently about them.

First of all, you want a tree that will do well; leave experimenting to the young gardeners. Stick with old favorites and standbys that are reliable performers. Decide whether you want year-round or seasonal flowers, tall shade trees or small trees near a terrace, colorful foliage in fall, or an evergreen for year-round beauty. After you decide on those factors, remember these four planning rules:

1. The tree must be in proportion to the other landscape material and to the size of the house.
2. Be sure the shape of the tree—mushroom, canopy, columnar—harmonizes with other planting materials.
3. Fit the tree to the best location.
4. Select the major shade trees first and then add the other trees that you want.

Care and Planting

The best tree to buy is young, dormant, and deciduous and ready to grow. As discussed in Chapter 3, trees at your nursery will be either balled and burlapped or in containers. No matter which you select, study it first to be sure it is the kind you want. Don't make snap decisions; look at many trees before making a final purchase.

Make the planting hole deep, about twice the size of the diameter of the root ball and at least half again as deep as the height of the root ball. Put a mound of soil in the bottom of the hole, and place the plant on it so that the crown is slightly above the soil line. Pour in water and let the soil settle. Next, fill the hole to the top with soil and form a water well around the plant. Fill the well a few times, and allow water to penetrate the soil. When you think you have added enough water, add some more.

For bare-root trees, follow the above planting suggestions and spread out roots; never bend, cut, or squeeze the roots into the hole.

Follow the same procedure for plants from containers but leave the root ball; be sure to leave the burlap on the tree roots with a B&B tree—cut it when the tree is in the soil. (The burlap will decay in time.)

In addition to watering, once trees are growing they will need pruning at specific times of the year. You can, of course, do some pruning yourself, but basically it pays to call in a professional. If you prune plants be sure to follow these hints:

- Remove Y-shaped crotches by cutting away the smaller of the two branches to stimulate the growth of the remaining branch and strengthen the wood.
- Shape trees as they are growing instead of waiting several years; drastic pruning (difficult work) will hurt both the tree and you.
- Stake trees with guy wires if necessary; a crooked tree is not pleasant to look at.
- Overgrown mature trees will need daylighting: thin and remove small branches so light can reach all parts of the tree. (Warning: this is strictly work for a professional.)
- Generally spring is the best time to feed a tree—feed every other watering with a mild fertilizer for about a month; later feeding is really not needed.

Here is a table of some deciduous and evergreen trees for your garden.

DECIDUOUS TREES

Botanical and Common Name	Approx. Height, Feet	Minimum Night Temp.	Remarks
Acer platanoides (Norway maple)	90	–35° to –20° F.	Grows rapidly
A. rubrum (red maple)	120	–35° to –20° F.	Best show in late spring
Aesculus x carnea (red horse chestnut)	60	–35° to –20° F.	No autumn color
Ailanthus altissima (tree-of-heaven)	60	–20° to –10° F.	Very adaptable
Albizzia julibrissin (silk tree)	20	–10° to –5° F.	Very ornamental
Betula pendula (European white birch)	60	–40° to –30° F.	Graceful but short lived
Carya ovata (shagbark hickory)	130	–30° to –10° F.	Narrow upright habit
Celtis occidentalis (hackberry)	75	–50° to –35° F.	Good shade tree
Cercis canadensis (eastern redbud)	26	–20° to –10° F.	Lovely flowers
Chionanthus virginica (fringe tree)	20	–20° to –10° F.	Bountiful flowers
Cornus florida (flowering dogwood)	25	–30° to –10° F.	Stellar ornamental
C. kousa (Japanese dogwood)	20	–10° to –5° F.	Lovely flowers in June
Crataegus mollis (downy hawthorn)	30	–20° to –10° F.	Pear-shaped red fruit

Botanical and Common Name	Approx. Height, Feet	Minimum Night Temp.	Remarks
Fagus grandifolia (American beech)	120	−35° to −20° F.	Stellar tree
F. sylvatica (European beech)	100	−20° to −10° F.	Several varieties
Fraxinus americana (White ash)	120	−35° to −20° F.	Grows in various soils
Ginkgo biloba (maidenhair tree)	120	−20° to −10° F.	Popular
Gleditsia triacanthos (sweet locust)	100	−20° to −10° F.	Several varieties
Koelreuteria paniculata (goldenrain tree)	30	−10° to −5° F.	Great summer bloom
Laburnum x watereri (golden-chain tree)	25	−10° to −5° F.	Deep-yellow flowers
Liquidambar styraciflua (sweet gum)	90	−10° to −5° F.	Beautiful symmetry
Magnolia soulangiana (saucer magnolia)	25	−10° to −5° F.	Many varieties; also evergreens, shrubs
M. stellata (starry magnolia)	20	−10° to −5° F.	Very ornamental
Malus baccata (Siberian crab apple)	45	−50° to −35° F.	Lovely flowers and fruit
M. floribunda (showy crab apple)	30	−20° to −10° F.	Handsome foliage and flowers
Populus alba (white poplar)	90	−35° to −20° F.	Spreading branches
Salix alba (white willow)	40	−50° to −35° F.	Good upright willow

Botanical and Common Name	Approx. Height, Feet	Minimum Night Temp.	Remarks
S. babylonica (weeping willow)	40	–10° to –5° F.	Fast grower
Tilia americana (American linden)	90	–50° to –35° F.	Fragrant white flowers in July
T. cordata (small-leaved linden)	60	–35° to –20° F.	Dense habit
T. tomentosa (silver linden)	80	–20° to –10° F.	Beautiful specimen tree
Ulmus americana (American elm)	100	–50° to –35° F.	Popular shade tree

EVERGREEN TREES

Botanical and Common Name	Approx. Height, Feet	Minimum Night Temp.	Remarks
Abies balsamea (balsam fir)	70	–35° to –20° F.	Handsome ornamental
Cedrus atlantica (atlas cedar)	100	–5° F.	Nice pyramid
Chamaecyparis obtusa (Hinoki cypress)	130	–20° to –10° F.	Broadly pyramidal
Cryptomeria japonica 'Lobbii' (Japanese cedar)	30 to 50	–5° F.	Pyramidal shape
Juniperus virginiana (red cedar)	30 to 50	–50° to –35° F.	Slow growing
Picea abies (*P. excelsa*) (Norway spruce)	75	–50° to –35° F.	Not for small grounds
Pinus bungeana (lacebark pine)	75	–20° to –10° F.	Slow growing

Botanical and Common Name	Approx. Height, Feet	Minimum Night Temp.	Remarks
P. densiflora (Japanese red pine)	80	−20° to −10° F.	Flattop habit
P. nigra (Austrian pine)	90	−20° to −10° F.	Fast growing
P. parviflora (Japanese white pine)	90	−10° to −5° F.	Handsome ornamental
Taxus baccata (English yew)	60	−5° to 5° F.	Best among yews
T. cuspidata 'Capitata' (Japanese yew)	50	−20° to −10° F.	Good landscape tree
Thuja occidentalis (American arborvitae)	65	−50° to −35° F.	Sometimes needles turn brown in winter
Tsuga canadensis (hemlock)	75	−35° to −20° F.	Many uses: hedges, screens, landscapes
T. caroliniana (Carolina hemlock)	75	−20° to −10° F.	Fine all-purpose evergreen
T. diversifolia (Japanese hemlock)	90	−10° to −5° F.	Smaller than most hemlocks

SHRUBS

Shrubs come in many shapes, sizes, and leaf textures and are definitely necessary in almost any attractive garden. The deciduous shrubs provide wild splashes of color, and the evergreens supply year-round beauty. The forms of these plants can be spreading, round topped, low, or high. Try to fit the plant to the area so it becomes a total part of the composition; shrubs should be used in broad brush strokes rather than as an accent here or there.

Buying and Planting

Like trees, shrubs are sold B&B, in containers, or bare root. Deciduous types, which lose their leaves in winter, are available during their dormant season for spring planting. Broad-leaved shrubs and evergreens (narrow-leaved) are available in containers or B&B at planting time.

Dig deep large holes for shrubs, and spread out the roots as you put them in the planting pockets. Break up the soil in the bottom of the hole, and add some topsoil so the plants can prosper. Always set shrubs in the ground at the same level they were at the nursery. Spacing shrubs is a touchy subject among gardeners; some put a 2-foot shrub about 12 feet from the next shrub. Other gardeners space plants every 6 feet; I am one of these because I am always eager for the garden to look complete and lovely.

If you use shrubs in hedges, remember that they will need clipping periodically to keep them attractive. Hedges may be tall or low, deciduous or evergreen, low growing or rigid, clipped or unclipped. For easy maintenance choose natural compact shrubs that are easy to prune; some shrubs will always look shaggy if clipped.

Plant hedge shrubs the way you would regular shrubs, but be sure to get them in a straight line: stretch a string along the spot to be planted, and mark a line on the ground. Plant evergreen hedges in fall or spring and deciduous ones in spring. Don't fertilize hedges too much or you'll have to trim them more frequently.

A list of shrubs follows.

SHRUBS

Botanical and Common Name	Approx. Height, Feet	Minimum Night Temp.	Remarks
Abelia x grandiflora (glossy abelia)	5	–10° to –5° F.	Free-flowering
Abeliophyllum distichum (Korean white forsythia)	3–4	–10° to –5° F.	Prune after bloom
Andromeda polifolia (bog rosemary)	1–2	–50° to –35° F.	Likes moist locations
Berberis koreana (Korean barberry)	2–10	–10° to –5° F.	Good outstanding colors; red berries
B. thunbergii (Japanese barberry)	7	–10° to –5° F.	Grows in any soil
Buddleia alternifolia (fountain buddleia)	12	–10° to –5° F.	Graceful; branching
B. davidii (butterfly bush)	15	–10° to –5° F.	Many varieties
Buxus microphylla japonica (Japanese boxwood)	4	–10° to –5° F.	Low and compact
B. microphylla koreana (Korean boxwood)	6–10	–20° to –10° F.	Hardiest; foliage turns brown in winter
Carpenteria californica (California mock orange)	8	5° to 20° F.	Showy shrub
Euonymus alata (winged euonymus)	9	–35° to –20° F.	Sturdy, easily grown
E. japonica (evergreen euonymus)	15	10° to 20° F.	Splendid foliage
E. latifolius	20	–10° to –5° F.	Vigorous grower

Botanical and Common Name	Approx. Height, Feet	Minimum Night Temp.	Remarks
Forsythia x intermedia (border forsythia)	2–9	–20° to –5° F.	Deep-yellow flowers
F. ovata (early forsythia)	8	–20° to –10° F.	Earliest to bloom and hardiest
Fothergilla major (large fothergilla)	9	–10° to –5° F.	Good flowers and autumn color
Gardenia jasminoides (Cape jasmine)	4–6	10° to 30° F.	Fragrant
Hamamelis vernalis (spring witch hazel)	10	–10° to –5° F.	Early spring blooms
Hydrangea arborescens 'Grandiflora' (hills-of-snow)	3	–20° to –10° F.	Easy culture
Ilex cornuta (Chinese holly)	9	5° to 10° F.	Bright berries; lustrous foliage
Ilex crenata (Japanese holly)	20	–5° to 5° F.	Another good holly
Jasminum nudiflorum (winter jasmine)	15	–10° to –5° F.	Viny shrub; not fragrant
J. officinale (common white jasmine)	30	5° to 10° F.	Tall-growing
Juniperus chinensis 'Pfitzeriana' (Pfitzer juniper)	10	–20° to –10° F.	Popular juniper
Kalmia latifolia (mountain laurel)	30	–20° to –10° F.	Amenable grower
Mahonia aquifolium (Oregon grape)	3–5	–10° to –5° F.	Handsome foliage
Pieris floribunda (mountain andromeda)	5	–20° to –10° F.	Does well in dry soil

Botanical and Common Name	Approx. Height, Feet	Minimum Night Temp.	Remarks
P. japonica (Japanese andromeda)	9	–10° to –5° F.	Splendid color
Potentilla fruticosa (cinquefoil)	2–5	–50° to –35 ° F.	Many varieties
Spiraea x arguta	6	–20° to –10° F.	Free-flowering
S. prunifolia (bridal wreath spiraea)	9	–20° to –10° F.	Turns orange in fall
S. thunbergii (thunberg spiraea)	5	–20° to –10° F.	Arching branches
S. veitchii	12	–10° to –5° F.	Background; graceful
Syringa villosa (late lilac)	9	–50° to –35° F.	Dense, upright habit
S. vulgaris (common lilac)	20	–35° to –20° F.	Many varieties
Viburnum davidii	3	5° to 10° F.	Handsome leaves
V. dentatum (arrowwood)	15	–50° to –35° F.	Red fall color
V. opulus (European cranberry bush)	12	–35° to –20° F.	Many varieties
V. prunifolium (black haw)	15	–35° to –20° F.	Good specimen plant
V. sieboldii	30	–20° to –10° F.	Stellar performer
V. trilobum (cranberry bush)	12	–50° to –35° F.	Effective in winter
Weigela 'Bristol Ruby'	7	–10° to –5° F.	Complex hybrid
Weigela 'Bristol Snowflake'	7	–10° to –5° F.	Complex hybrid
Weigela florida	9	–10° to –5° F.	Many available

BULBS

For easy, no-bend gardening, bulbs are a sheer delight. The plant is already in the bulb and merely needs planting and watering to bring a wealth of color to your garden. The new bulb planters—those with long handles—eliminate bending and there is no pruning, weeding, or battling with bugs when you plant bulbs.

Many of the most beautiful bulb flowers are winter hardy and thus can be left in the ground year after year; they need cold weather to grow. Other bulbs must be planted and lifted each year— these are the ones to avoid because uprooting and replanting means additional labor in early spring, when there are so many other gardening chores to do. But although we shall list the winter-hardy bulbs here, those with more energy and youth can certainly grow the other bulbs also.

Planting

Generally, most bulbs need a moisture-retentive and rapid-draining soil of high organic matter. Dig round holes with a concave bottom because pointed holes leave an air pocket below the bulb. Some debate exists about which end of the bulb to put into the ground. When figuring the depth at which to plant a bulb, remember a 3-inch depth means that the bulb has its top, not its bottom, 3 inches below the ground level. Firm the soil around the bulb rather than leaving it loose.

Buy the best bulbs you can afford from *reputable* dealers. Because you are buying an unseen product, you must trust the dealer's reputation rather than your eye.

Bulbs have their own storehouse of food, but they cannot grow indefinitely without some help from you. In active growth be sure to water them regularly, and after flowers have faded continue watering to ripen the next year's growth.

There are hardy spring-flowering bulbs and summer-flowering ones. A list of each type follows.

BULBS
Spring-flowering Bulbs

Botanical and Common Name	When to Plant	Depth, Inches	Sun or Shade	Remarks
Allium (flowering onion)	Fall	3	Sun	Prettier than you think
Chionodoxa (glory-of-snow)	Fall	3	Sun	Do not disturb for several years
Crocus	Fall	3	Sun	Always dependable
Daffodil (jonquil, narcissus)	Fall	6	Sun	The name "daffodil" is used for all members
Eranthis (winter aconite)	Early fall	3	Shade	Very early bloom
Erythronium (dogtooth violet)	Early fall	6	Shade	Good for naturalizing
Fritillaria	Fall	4	Shade	Overlooked but lovely
Galanthus (snowdrop)	Fall	3	Shade	Blooms while snow is on the ground
Hyacinthus (hyacinth)	Fall	6–8	Sun	Protect from wind and mice
Leucojum (snowflake)	Fall	3	Shade	Flowers last a long time
Muscari (grape hyacinth)	Early fall	3	Sun	Easy to grow
Scilla	Fall	2	Sun or light shade	Once established, blooms indefinitely
Tulipa (tulip)	Fall	10–12	Sun	Needs cold winters

BULBS
Summer-flowering Bulbs

Botanical and Common Name	Depth, Inches	Sun or Shade	Remarks
Agapanthus (flower-of-the-Nile)	1	Sun	New dwarf varieties available
Alstroemeria	4	Sun	Good cut flowers
Begonia (tuberous)	4	Shade	Lovely flowers; many varieties
Canna	2	Sun	Lift bulbs after frost kills tops
Dahlia	3–4	Sun	Needs excellent drainage
Galtonia (summer hyacinth)	6	Sun	Buy new bulbs yearly
Gladiolus (gladiola)	4–6	Sun	Likes copious watering
Iris	4–6	Sun	Many different kinds
Lilium (lily)	4–8	Sun	Best in second year
Polianthes tuberosa (Tuberose)	1	Sun	Plant after danger of frost
Ranunculus	1	Sun	Lovely colorful flowers
Sprekelia formosissima (Jacobean lily)	3	Sun	Good in pots
Tigridia (tiger flower)	2–3	Sun	Plant in early May
Tritonia (montbretia)	2–3	Sun	Plant in early May
Zephyranthes (zephyr lily)	1	Sun or light shade	Plant after danger of frost

CHAPTER EIGHT

How to Kill Insects without Killing Yourself

Y ears ago, sprays and dusts, chemicals and equipment were part of the gardener's artillery against insect attack, but now there is a better way of combating destructive culprits in the garden: organic gardening. Organic gardening utilizes nature's preventatives, birds and insects, and doesn't involve poisonous chemicals that can kill the good birds and insects along with the bad ones. (And once destroyed, the natural ecology can't be reestablished for quite a while.) Gardening with nature also involves using natural preventatives such as old-fashioned laundry soap and water and botanical sprays.

ENCOURAGING BIRDS

The most common birds in your garden are liable to be good ones that will keep plants almost insect free. (There are a few birds that will, unfortunately, eat berries and fruits along with their basic diet of insects.) Adult birds also keep their young supplied with insects; at certain times young birds need more than their own weight in food daily.

I bless birds. It's far easier to have the birds control insects than for me to drag out spray cans and apparatus and further contaminate the air with what may be dubious poisons. Birds can be encouraged to visit our gardens if we issue the proper invitation.

ATTRACTING BIRDS

Attract birds with food, protection, bird feeders, and landscaping. (Certain shrubs and trees provide birds with a nesting place and insects to eat.)

Water is also a compelling attraction—birds love to play in it, and in regions where it does not rain for many weeks water for drinking is essential to birds. Birds like shallow or deep bird baths or a mist of water. The following plants help bring birds to the garden:

Shrubs	Trees	Vines
Bayberry	Alder	Bittersweet
Blackhaw	Ash	Greenbrier
Buckthorn	Beech	Hall's honeysuckle
Cranberry	Birch	Virginia creeper
Dogwood	Flowering crab	Wild grape
Elderberry	Flowering dogwood	
Honeysuckle	Hawthorn	
Inkberry	Linden	
Japanese barberry	Maple	
Winterberry	Mulberry	
	Norway spruce	
	Oak	
	Red cedar	
	White spruce	

FEEDING BIRDS

Birds may also need supplemental feeding added to their natural diet of insects. In summer, there is usually enough food for them (unless there is little or no vegetation), but when natural food becomes scarce in winter, feeding is beneficial. Once you start feeding birds you must continue; they rely on you. (There is quite a ruckus on my porch when I forget to feed the birds.)

Select one of the many commercial feeders and locate it close to the house. Insect-eating birds eat many adult insects as well as their larvae. Avoid suet (a perfect substitute for larvae) so birds will work for their keep. Don't overfeed in the summer.

THE BEST BIRDS

Some birds, such as chickadees, house wrens, towhees, and phoebes, are better than others for controlling and eating insects.

Swallows rely almost entirely on insects for food; the purple martin swallow is perhaps the most useful in the garden. Baltimore orioles eat caterpillars, beetles, ants, grasshoppers, and click beetles; cuckoos devour hairy caterpillars, beetles, grasshoppers, sawflies, some spiders, tent caterpillars, and crickets. The kingbird is invaluable because he eats almost all kinds of destructive pests. Woodpeckers, although sometimes annoying, eat wood-boring beetles and fruitwood insects; towhees feast on hibernating beetles and larvae. And meadowlarks will also eat some weeds from the lawn as well as bugs.

Mockingbirds, grosbeaks, and to some extent, members of the sparrow family (e.g. the junco) also eat fruit. The linnet or house finch can be a pest too, and common jays chase away other, more beneficial birds. Helpful birds are:

Baltimore oriole	Kingfisher
Barn swallow	Meadowlark
Brown thrasher	Mockingbird
Catbird	Phoebe
Cedar waxwing	Purple martin
Common nighthawk	Song sparrow
Downy woodpecker	Tufted titmouse
Eastern kingbird	Woodthrush
House wren	

INSECTS

Some insects are also superb garden protectors. Called predators, they feed on other destructive insects. Ladybugs (beetles) are efficient insects. They are veritable aphid-eating machines: the

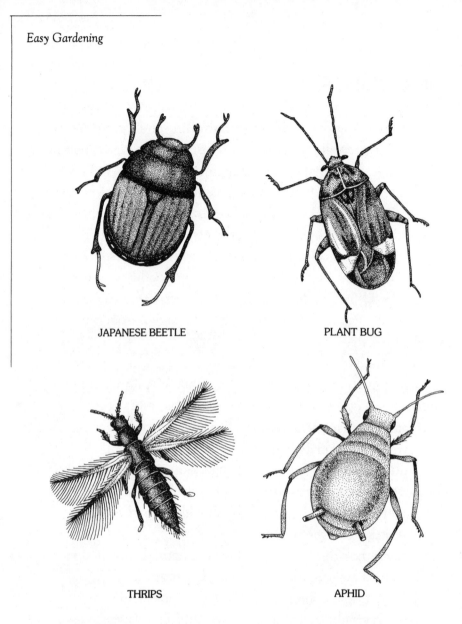

JAPANESE BEETLE

PLANT BUG

THRIPS

APHID

(Drawing by B. Johnson)

average ladybug (there are about 350 species in the United States) can consume 400 insects a week. The convergent lady beetle is well suited for insect control because it can be collected in its hibernation state.

If nature hasn't been upset on your property, ladybugs will

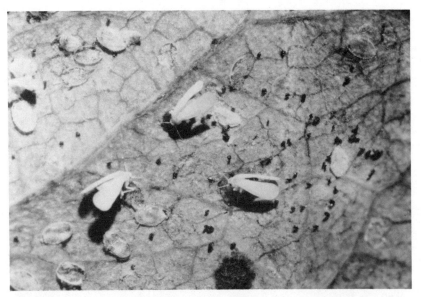

Whiteflies can be a pest in the garden and suitable remedies must be taken. Sometimes repeated heavy dousings with a hose does it. (Photo by USDA)

arrive with the first warm weather. But if you have used chemical sprays, you can get ladybugs from suppliers; simply "plant" them in your garden. They come in convenient cases and can be left in their cases for a few days. Place a little water in the box and put it in the refrigerator. To put ladybugs in the garden, dampen the soil and set them out near food (aphids).

Among the aphis lions (lacewings, ant lions, dobson flies, etc.) the nocturnal lacewings are the best garden controllers; they feed on scale insects, thrips, aphids, mealybugs, moth eggs, and caterpillars. The green lacewing (called golden eyes) and their larvae are both welcome in my garden because they eat aphids, red spiders, and thrips. You can find the larvae of the brown lacewing (called aphis wolves) stuck to the undersides of leaves or on the bark of trees.

Ant lions (doodlebugs) trap their prey by digging a pit, burying themselves at the bottom, and waiting for unwary victims to fall in. Ant lions can destroy quite a number of ants in a single season.

The ambush bug inhabits mainly flowering plants and hides behind foliage or blossoms and then grabs its victims. Don't kill these ugly bugs; they have a pair of highly developed front legs that they use for grabbing, and they eat many pests.

The predatory assassin bug, which has a bite as painful as the sting of a wasp, isn't completely beneficial in the garden, but it does have its uses. Damsel bugs are ideal in the garden because they consume aphids, mites, caterpillars, and so forth.

The praying mantises are extremely beneficial and won't leave your property if they have enough insects to eat. When young

Close-up of mealy bugs in action; this plant is beyond recovery. Try to catch mealy bugs early and they can be eradicated with a soap-and-water solution. (Photo by author)

they eat mainly such soft-bodied insects as aphids and leafhoppers; when they are mature their diet includes tent caterpillars, chinch bugs, beetles, and other insects.

You can buy egg cases of mantises between November and May. (Figure on about five cases per half acre.) Tie or tape one case to a shrub or tree, at least 2 to 4 feet above the ground. The cases will survive during the cold months, and the mantises will emerge sometime in June or July.

Hover flies are quite useful; the larvae of some species feed on aphids, and others love mealybugs and leafhoppers. Tachinid flies are also beneficial because they control caterpillars, cutworms, and armyworms. However, it is difficult to protect these beneficial flies because they look like the ordinary, nonpredatory flies.

Spiders belong to the class *Arachnida*, so they aren't true insects—they have four pairs of legs, versus insects' three pairs, and don't have antennae or wings. But many spiders are useful in the garden. In fact, some authorities consider spiders among the dominant predators of the earth. Spiders thrive on live insects. They control pine sawflies and tobacco budworm.

NATURAL PREVENTATIVES

Predatory insects and birds will, to a great extent, help to keep the garden generally pest free. But there are other natural defenses that are simple and easy that we can use too. These include companion planting, botanical repellants, and some good old-fashioned remedies that many of us remember.

Any garden with a concentration of one particular plant is an invitation to insects. However, if you mix your plantings or companion-plant, as it is called, there will be a lesser chance of pests invading your garden. Tansy, a pretty herb, discourages cutworms, cabbageworms, and slugs. Rue is a hardy evergreen plant that some insects will avoid (along with the plants growing near

Dunking infected plants in a bucket of laundry soap and water helps eliminate many pests. (Photo by author)

it); marigolds and asters also deter insects to some degree. But the most popular plants that repel are garlic and chives. Certainly these are easily grown and are not objectionable in the flower garden. Just what is the repellant quality of these plants? With most of them the leaves have a disagreeable odor or a bitter taste.

As mentioned, chemical sprays should be avoided in the garden. However, botanical insecticides—pyrethum, rotenone, quassia, and ryania—are not persistent and are not harmful to man or earth. They are made from various plants and are now available as packaged insecticides.

Pyrethum kills aphids, white flies, leafhoppers, and thrips on contact. Rotenone wards off spider mites, chinch bugs, aphids, and the common housefly. Ryania, although not lethal, incapacitates (perhaps by paralysis) Japanese beetles, elm leaf beetles, and cabbage loopers. More and more of the chemical companies that

The venerable ladybug eats aphids and other plant pests. Natural preventatives are an excellent way of protecting plants and can be purchased at specialty mail-order firms. (Photo by Joyce Wilson)

formerly used deadly poisons for garden protection are now marketing these natural controls. However, check contents on packages carefully to be sure persistent poisons are not added.

Before leaving botanical insecticides let us look at a very old one—nicotine—which is available as nicotine sulfate. This is a poisonous alkaloid for insects and it is highly toxic to mammals, including humans. However, it dissipates rapidly and is effective against aphids, white fly, leafhoppers, and dozens of other pests. If your garden is attacked by a heavy infestation of insects (and this would be rare), you can occasionally use the nicotine solution if you deem it necessary.

If you can bring yourself to touch insects, handpicking is still an effective way of ridding the small garden of pests. This of course will work for large insects, but for pests such as aphids and spider mites you can resort to the old-fashioned solution of laundry soap and water. Use a half pound of laundry soap to 2 gallons of water, spray plants, and then hose them with clear water. This preparation will also eliminate red spiders, mealybugs, and scale. Don't expect a miracle though, it takes several sprayings to really beat the insects, but it is well worth the trouble in order to avoid the use of poisons.

CHAPTER NINE

Your Indoor Garden

I ndoor gardens—whether on a window sill or in a window box—are our winter retreats, the bridge from fall to spring, and I wouldn't want to be without houseplants. Through the years I have grown an array of indoor beauties, but because outside gardening has occupied me recently and I have tried to cut my gardening—indoors and outdoors—I have eventually eliminated the difficult houseplants and concentrated on those that thrive almost by themselves.

I have found that most plants (if given proper light conditions) will respond with lush leaves and bountiful bloom; it is these plants we shall discuss. We won't discuss plants under artificial light because of a lack of space, but this is a fine hobby, and there are many good books about the subject. Those that demand constant attention and are temperamental (e.g. *Dizygotheca*) are too much trouble. I want plants, and I think you might too, that offer the most for least effort.

MINIMUM MAINTENANCE PLANTS

A minimum maintenance houseplant is a plant that can grow with nominal watering—about twice a week—and occasional repotting and pruning and still be attractive. Bromeliads and orchids (yes, orchids) are plants that can, if necessary, take care of themselves. Some bromeliads have built-in vaselike reservoirs that hold water, and orchids have pseudobulbs that see them through drought in case you forget to water them. Ferns and palms are other fine candidates for the gardener who wants a lot for a little care. And aglaonemas, begonias, geraniums, and gesneriads are other

This bay window garden hosts many plants; there are cacti, philodendron, dradracaena, handsome additions to any room. (Photo by Matthew Barr)

good plants for the indoor greenery. Cacti and succulents are often overlooked, but they are ideal for indoor decoration.

AVOID THE DIFFICULT PLANTS

It doesn't make much sense to grow difficult plants when there are so many "easy" plants available. Ironically, philodendrons, long classified as excellent house plants, are anything but amenable indoor subjects because they are naturally vining plants not used to confining pots. After a few months they look straggly and must be replaced. Dieffenbachias are other reluctant indoor performers; in the slightest draft they become a disaster as do the rubber plants and fiddle-leaf fig. In spite of their popularity, African violets are apt to be somewhat fussy too, although newer varieties bred for better bloom and robustness are now appearing.

HOUSEPLANT CULTURE

Houseplants are either cool growing (60° to 65° F. by day) or warm growing (75° to 80° F. by day). Although plants will tolerate temperature differences, they all need light and won't grow or live without it. Some plants require sun—an east or south window—others need a bright western exposure, and many foliage plants prosper in northern light. So select your plants accordingly.

Almost all living rooms provide humidity or air moisture of 30 to 40 percent, which is adequate for most plants. Humidity can be increased in various ways for species requiring more; this is discussed later in the chapter. Fresh air and good ventilation are also essential to plant health, even in very cold weather, but too often plants are relegated to stuffy atmospheres.

Soil

I use one part garden loam to one part sand to one part leaf mold for most plants. For cacti and succulents I allow almost one-half instead of one-third sand. Orchids and bromeliads need osmunda (chopped roots of various ferns) or fir bark (steamed pieces of evergreen bark); both can be obtained in small sacks at nurseries.

Commercially packaged soil, usually rather heavy, is good for some plants, but not for all. Usually you can buy a better soil mixture by the bushel from a greenhouse (and this will be the same soil they use). It is sterilized and contains all the necessary ingredients. (Generally, avoid garden soils because they contain weeds, seeds, insect grubs, and bacteria that can cause disease in plants.) Use the soil mixture as is, or alter it according to the needs of your own plants. If it is not porous enough, add more sand; if it feels thin, put in more leaf mold or compost.

Growing mediums that contain no soil have been developed by Cornell University; they are called peatlite mixes. For one peck, combine:

4 quarts, dry measure, vermiculite
4 quarts, dry measure, shredded peatmoss
1 level tablespoon of ground limestone
1 level tablespoon 5-10-5 fertilizer

I have found this medium excellent for seedlings, but for tubbed plants you must give supplemental feeding of a water-soluble fertilizer every other watering through the growing season, which is tedious work.

Potting and Repotting

Potting refers to the first planting of a seedling or cutting in a container; repotting refers to the transfer of a plant from one pot to another, usually larger, one. For good growth, give plants proper potting. Select a container neither too large nor too small in relation to the size of a specimen.

When potting a plant, be sure the container is clean. Soak new clay pots overnight in water before using them or they will draw undue moisture from the soil of new plantings. Scrub old pots with steelwool soap pads and hot water to remove any algae or salt accumulation.

Fit an arching piece or two of broken pot (shards) over the drainage hole. Place the plant in the center of the pot, and fill in and around it with fresh soil mixture. Hold the plant in position with one hand, and fill soil in and around it with the other. Firm soil around the stem with your thumbs. To settle the soil and

In a small area indoor plants afford a fine place for greenery and provide the grower hours of pleasure. (Photo by author)

eliminate air spaces, strike the base of the pot on a table a few times. A properly potted plant can be lifted by the stem without being loosened.

Leave about an inch of space at the top between pot rim and soil so the plant can receive water. Water newly potted plants thoroughly, and then for a few days keep them in a light but not a sunny place. Once accustomed to brightness they can be moved. Label all plants; it's nice to know what you're growing.

It is time to give roots more room and to replenish the soil when roots push through the drainage hole of a pot or appear on the surface. An exact schedule for repotting is not possible; instead, consider the needs of each plant. If you fertilize regularly, thus replacing soil nutrients, plants thrive in the same pot longer than if they are not fed.

Watering and Feeding

How and when you water depends on the type of pot used, where you live, and the kind of plant. Never allow any plant to go completely dry (even during semidormancy), and never keep one in soggy soil. If soil is too dry, plant roots become dehydrated and growth stops; continuously wet soil becomes sour and roots rot.

Some plants prefer an evenly moist soil, but others, like begonias and clivias, grow best in soil that is allowed to approach dryness between waterings. Cacti and some other succulents may be permitted to become almost completely dry.

Water *thoroughly*. Allow excess water to pour from the drainage hole; the complete root system needs moisture. If only the top soil gets wet and the lower part stays dry, the soil usually turns sour and growth is retarded.

Water at room temperature is best. If possible, water in the morning so the soil can dry out before evening. Lingering moisture and cool nights are an invitation to fungus diseases.

Most plants benefit from adding fertilizer; however, bromeliads and other flowering plants do not need it. Commercial fertilizers contain some nitrogen, an element that stimulates foliage growth, but too much can retard development of flower buds. Fertilizers also contain phosphorus, which promotes root and stem development and stimulates bloom, and potash, which promotes health, stabilizes growth, and intensifies color. The ratio of elements is marked on the package or bottle in this order: nitrogen, phosphorus, potash. There are many formulas; I prefer 10-10-5 for most house plants.

New and ailing plants do not require fertilizing. New ones in fresh soil have adequate nutrients and do not need more; ailing plants may not be capable of absorbing nutrients and when growing slowly do not need added nutrients. After they flower, allow plants to rest for a few weeks; water only occasionally and do not feed. A safe rule is to fertilize only the plants that are in active growth.

Heat and Humidity

Plants like campanulas and hoyas prefer coolness (54° to 58° F. at night, 10° to 15° F. more during the day). Warm-growers like anthuriums and most begonias require 64° to 68° F. at night, 72° to 80° F. during the day. With few exceptions (indicated in the plant list later in the chapter), most plants fall into one of these groups. In other words, average home temperatures suit most plants.

In winter, it's necessary to protect plants from extreme cold. Put cardboard or newspapers between plants and windows to mitigate the chill of the glass on very cold nights.

Although automatic humidifiers are now part of many heating systems, older apartment houses and buildings don't have them. Humidity—the amount of moisture in the air—should be at a healthful level for both people and plants. A humidity gauge (a hydrometer) registers the amount of relative humidity. Thirty to 40 percent is average for most homes and good for most plants. However, some plants, such as clivia and philodendron, will grow in a low humidity—about 30 percent; other plants, like rechsteinerias and gloxinias, require humidity of 60 to 70 percent.

It is hard to keep humidity in the proper relation to artificial and summer heat. The hotter it is, the faster air dries out. Because plants take up water through roots and release it through leaves, they give off moisture faster when the surrounding air is dry rather than damp. If plants use water quicker than they can replace it, foliage becomes thin and depleted. When summer heat is at its peak (between 11:00 A.M and 1:00 P.M.), spray plants lightly with water. For years, a 15-cent window-cleaning bottle was essential equipment for me, but today's new sprayers give better misting than my old-fashioned gadget. Made under various trade names, these hand-operated fog makers have a plastic, noncorrosive, washable container and come in 16- or 32-ounce sizes. They dispense a fine mist that is beneficial to almost all plants because they cleanse the foliage and, for a brief time anyway, increase the humidity.

In winter, when artificial heat is high (between 8:00 A.M. and 8:00 P.M.), provide more air moisture. Turn on your room humidifier or mist pots and soil surface but not foliage; at night wet foliage is an invitation to disease.

In addition to misting, set plants on wet gravel in a large metal or fiberglass tray about 3 inches deep. This furnishes a good amount of additional humidity. You can also place plants on pebble-filled saucers; keep stones constantly moist. But for best results, use an inexpensive space-humidifier that operates on a small motor; it breaks water into minute particles and diffuses it through the atmosphere.

A group of bromeliads—easy-to-care-for plants—on a windowsill. Plants are set on gravel in metal (or plastic) pans. (Photo by author)

Strong growth and firm leaves (assuming temperature and light are in proper proportion) are signs of good humidity. Spindly growth and limp leaves usually indicate too little moisture in the air. Keep plants away from hot radiators and blasts of hot air and out of drafts.

A list of houseplants follows.

IDEAL HOUSEPLANTS

Plant	Size	Time of Bloom	Summer Outdoors	Exposure	Remarks
Acalypha hispida (chenille plant)	S	May		S	Temporary plant
Aechmea angustifolia	M	Feb.–May	*	L	Blue berries
A. calyculata	M	Nov.–Mar.	*	Sh	Pot offshoots when three inches high
A. chantinii	L	Mar.–June	*	L	Perhaps the best
A. fasciata	M	Sept.–Jan.	*	Sh	Stays colorful for six months
Aeschynanthus specious	V	June–Aug.		L	Keep potbound
Aglaonema commutatum	M	Dec.		Sh	Avoid repotting; top-dress
Allophyton mexicanum	S	Sept.	*	S	Worth a try
Anthurium scherzerianum	S	Jan.–Apr.		Sh	Grow warm with humidity
Aphelandra aurantiaca 'Roezlii'	S	June		L	Needs good air circulation
Asparagus sprengeri	L	Jan.		Sh	Spray foliage with water frequently
Begonia 'alleryi'	S	Nov.–Mar.		L	Easy to grow
B. 'Bow-Arriola'	S	Jan.		L	Grow quite dry
B. 'Elsie M. Frey'	V	Oct.		L	Basket type
B. 'Limminghei'	V	Jan.–May		L	Grow warm
B. x ricinifolia	M	May–Aug.		L	Robust plant
Beloperone guttata (shrimp plant)	M	Oct.–Nov.	*	L	Prune in spring

Plant	Size	Time of Bloom	Summer Outdoors	Exposure	Remarks
Billbergia nutans	L	Jan.	*	S	Grow as specimen
Brassavola nodosa	S	Sept.–Oct.		S	Dry out in August
Capsicum annuum	S	Nov.		S	The pepper plant
Ceropegia barkleyi	V	Nov.–Dec.		L	Somewhat difficult
C. woodii	V	Dec.		L	Keep on dry side
Chlorophytum elatum	L	Jan.		Sh	Stands abuse
Clerodendrum thomsoniae	L	June		L	Best of group
Clivia miniata	L	Apr.		Sh	Grow quite dry for bloom
Coelogyne cristata	S	Feb.		L	Grow cool in November
Columnea arguta	V	Apr.–July		L	Keep in small pots
C. hirta	V	Apr.–July		L	Keep in small pots
Costus igneus	S	July–Aug.		L	A real beauty
Crossandra infundibuliformis	M	Apr.–Aug.		L	Requires good air circulation
Dendrobium pierardii	M	Mar.–May		L	Keep somewhat dry after bloom
Dipladenia x amoena (*Mandevilla x amabilis*)	M	June		L	Short rest after flowering

Plant	Size	Time of Bloom	Summer Outdoors	Exposure	Remarks
Episcia cupreata	V	July–Aug.		L	At best in baskets
E. lilacina	V	July–Aug.		L	At best in baskets
Eucharis grandiflora (Amazon lily)	M	Apr.	*	L	Watch for mealybugs
Eucomis punctata (*E. comosa*) (pineapple flower)	M	July–Aug.	*	S	Grows from bulb
Euphorbia pulcherrima (*Poinsettia*)	L	Dec.–Jan.		L	The Christmas poinsettia
E. splendens (crown of thorns)	S	Feb.–Apr.	*	L	Grow on the dry side
Gloriosa rothschildiana	V	July–Aug.	*	Sh	Popular tuber plant
Gloxinia (*Sinningia*)	M	June		L	Keep foliage dry
Hoya bella (wax plant)	V	Sept.–Oct.		Sh	Popular wax plant, miniature form
Kaempferia roscoeana	S	June		L	A flower a day in summer
Kalanchoe blossfeldiana	M	Dec.		S	Grow quite dry
Kohleria amabilis	S	June	*	L	Warmth and humidity
K. bogotensis	M	July	*	L	Warmth and humidity
Lantana montevidensis	V	Feb.–Apr.		L	Superior basket plant

Plant	Size	Time of Bloom	Summer Outdoors	Exposure	Remarks
Lycaste aromatica	M	Oct.–Nov.		Sh	Dry out plant severely after flowering
Manettia bicolor	S	Jan.–Mar.		L	Keep potbound
Medinilla magnifica	L	Jan.	*	L	Only mature plants bloom
Musa nana (dwarf banana)	L	Mar.	*	Sh	Pot up offshoots
Neoregelia carolinae	L	Oct.–Feb.	*	Sh	Color for seven months
Nerium oleander	M	June	*	L	Leaves poisonous
Plumbago capensis	L	July–Aug.	*	L	Grow somewhat dry for bloom
Punica granatum 'Nana'	S	Oct.		L	Good year-round plant
Rechsteineria leucotricha	S	July–Aug.		S	Rest after flowering
Rhipsalis burchelli	M	Jan.		S	Humidity and warmth
Ruellia macrantha	M	Nov.–Jan.	*	Sh	Bushy
Solanum pseudo-capsicum (Jerusalem cherry)	S	Dec.		S	Temporary houseplant
Sprekelia formosissima	M	Apr.	*	S	Grow crowded
Stephanotis floribunda (Madagascar jasmine)	V	Apr.	*	L	Give winter rest
Streptocarpus rexii	M	Apr.–July		Sh	Water carefully in winter

Plant	Size	Time of Bloom	Summer Outdoors	Exposure	Remarks
Tibouchina semidecandra	S	May–Sept.	*	S	Prune and pinch
Vallota speciosa	M	May		S	Grow dry after flowering
Veltheimia viridifolia	L	Dec.		S	Grow dry after flowering

Size

S   (small): to twenty-four inches.

M   (medium): twenty-four to thirty-six inches.

L   (large): thirty-six inches and over.

V   vine.

Exposure

S   (sun): three to four hours.

L   (bright light): two or three hours.

Sh   (semishade): one to two hours.

*On porch or in garden for best results.

DWARF VEGETABLES

Do you like fresh vegetables but never thought you could have them, because you live in an apartment or your garden isn't big enough? Well, think again. With today's new midget vegetables, you can have a bonanza of crops in baskets in and around the kitchen: in windows, perhaps outdoors behind the kitchen area, or on the back porch. Cucumbers, green peppers, lettuce, and even tiny and delicious eggplant can decorate your house or apartment and be a ready food-supply larder.

Most midget vegetables—tomatoes, cucumbers, eggplant, green peppers—are available prestarted at your local nursery or dime store at the proper planting time. You can start your own plants from seed early in the season and transplant later, but this is time consuming. The prestarts are already growing; all you do is plant them in soil in a suitable pot. However, lettuce, radishes, and carrots are so easy to grow that you'll have to start them from seed. Just place them in a starting medium such as vermiculite, put them in bright light and warmth, and give them good humidity. (A baggie placed over the container and propped up on sticks solves this last problem.)

With vegetables, it's nonstop growing, so make sure you water them every morning. Once a week give them a plant food such as 10-10-5 to keep them moving along. Some vegetables are ready in 50 days, but others take up to 60 or 70 days.

Carrots

There's no comparison between homegrown carrots and the weeks-old ones from the supermarket. Especially good are the sweet and tender baby carrots. Carrots need a very friable, open soil to prosper. The longer it takes a carrot to mature, the more pithy it'll be, so feed and water frequently to encourage rapid growth. Carrots vary in length from 3 to 15 inches, so be sure to use the proper size container.

Sow carrot seeds in spring or fall, and don't fret if it takes a while; many varieties don't germinate for 3 to 4 weeks. Plant two rows of carrots, and thin them out when they're about 3 inches tall. Thin the plants again in about a month. Most varieties require about 70 days to mature. You can resow after harvesting if you want more carrots. Four good varieties are Baby Finger Nantes, Nantes, Short 'n' Sweet, and Tiny Sweet.

Lettuce

Growing your own lettuce is so simple. The loose-head leafy types are excellent for growing in containers and are ready for plucking within 50 days. Sow the seed where it is to mature, and protect plants against heat. Give them light, but direct sun isn't necessary to guarantee a crop. Have about six or eight plants to a container, and resow after harvesting each plant to insure a constant succession of good greens. Use a 10-10-5 fertilizer, and give lettuce sufficient quantities of water once it's growing. Although maturity time is 50 days, in about a month you can be eating the excellent "thinnings." When lettuce is mature, harvest the outer leaves along with a few inner ones at each cutting. Wash and eat the leaves; you'll be amazed at the flavor.

Besides being an easy crop to grow, lettuce makes a pretty pot plant that can even be used as a centerpiece—if you want to look and eat at the same time.

Excellent lettuce varieties include Bibb lettuce, Buttercrunch, Oak Leaf, salad bowl, and Tom Thumb Bibb.

Endive and Escarole

These zesty and delicious greens can be used with lettuce or eaten by themselves as a salad. Like lettuce, they're incredibly easy to grow, and two or three plants will furnish ample greens for the family. Pick leaves as you do with lettuce, or harvest the entire plant when it's mature. Plants need lots of water and a bright but not sunny spot. Use a 10-10-5 fertilizer. Thin them once or twice to give ample growing space for other seedlings. Within 40 to 50 days you should have a good crop. Green Curled endive and Full Heart Batavian escarole are good varieties.

Radishes

Radishes are for the rank beginner, because no matter how you grow them, they're invariably successful. They grow fast and bear abundantly—two prime requisites for the anxious city gardener. Radishes don't have to be transplanted, and can be sown in the same container they are to grow in. Even if you're all brown thumbs, you should have a crop within a month.

Generally, radishes don't like hot weather, so get them going early in spring. If you water the plants thoroughly, and I mean water them, the radishes will be crisp and tender: Fertilize them when first young leaves appear. How do you tell when the radishes are ready? Pick one—you'll have some to spare. They should be crisp and succulent, never pithy. Replace harvested ones with new seeds to have a succession of radishes. Named varieties are Champion radish, Cherry Belle radish, and Icicle.

Peppers

These attractive plants, with dark green foliage, can be grown easily in containers. Peppers need a warm growing period of about 4 months, with night temperatures never below 65° F. Planting can be started in April or May, depending upon your region. Harvest your peppers about 8 to 9 weeks after the first transplanting. Frequent harvesting will encourage production through the summer.

Try both the long and slender hot peppers and the succulent sweet bell peppers. The plants make bushy, 2- to 3-foot tall plants that are fine decoration for the kitchen.

Types to try are Burgess Michigan Wonder, Canape, and Italiana Sweet varieties.

Eggplant

A warm weather crop, eggplant does best at about 80° F. during the day and 68° F. at night. Start seeds in April or May, depending upon your location, and use peat pots, which do not have to be removed, to avoid shock of transplanting. When plants are ready for transplanting, use somewhat large containers. Eggplant needs a long, warm growing season, so put them outside on the porch or balcony when weather is uniformly warm. Keep them well watered and in a bright place.

Plants can be easily trained to a stake or trellis, and grow about 3 or 4 feet, depending upon the variety. As blossoms appear, remove some so the eggplant doesn't set too many fruits. Pinch back terminal stem growth to keep plant bushy. Eggplant should bear in about 75 to 90 days; harvest immediately, even when the fruits are half-size, because if picked too late, the fruit will have a bitter taste. Do try Black Magic, Golden Yellow, and Morden Midget.

Cucumbers

A few years ago, I first saw cucumbers growing in a container on a windowsill. I was amazed and amused to see tiny, delicious cucumbers grown as house plants. But cucumbers are extremely robust, grow quickly, and produce a good harvest. You can sow the midget variety seeds directly in soil in a large 12-inch container. Insert trellises or stakes so the plants can climb. Train the vine so the center becomes bushy and the lateral stems develop sideways.

Give plants plenty of water, and be sure to add some manure to the potting soil. Keep them in a bright place, although direct sun isn't necessary. Cucumbers start bearing in about 40 to 70 days and can be picked at any stage. The young ones will be tiny but ideal for sweet pickles; larger ones, if you let them mature, are fine for salads. Try Challenger Hybrid, China Hybrid, Mincu, Patio Pick, Triumph Hybrid, and Victory Slicing.

Onions and Chives

Most people aren't inclined to grow onions because they're not a popular cooked vegetable dish. Nor are they used overabundantly in salads. But you, the home grower, are missing a bet if you don't harvest scallions (those sweet-tasting green onions) or chives; they're very easy plants to tend and well worth their space.

You can buy sets or plants of scallions; just place them 1 inch apart in a 10-inch pot. Plants will be ready for eating in about 3 weeks, at which time you should harvest every other one, leaving the remaining ones room to grow. Plenty of water and good sun will bring onions to perfection.

Chives grow quite easily and are the most agreeable of plants, needing only even moisture and good light to keep producing. Simply snip tops of chives to garnish soups and salads and to season gravies. There are really no superior varieties; all seem good, so pick from your mail-order catalog or from what is available in little pots at your local supermarket.

Tomatoes

Few things beat the sweet luscious taste of freshly picked tomatoes. Luckily, tomatoes are perhaps the easiest vegetable for the neophyte gardener to grow. There are varieties specifically bred for container growing, and plants are strong and resistant to diseases. You can start your own plants from seed, but there's a good selection of prestarted seedlings at nurseries.

Tomatoes need warm temperatures and as much sun as possible to produce a good crop. Set the pots on balconies, porches, or outdoor windowsills. Tomatoes are climbers, and so need to be staked; insert trellises or wood stakes into the soil, and fasten plants with tie-ons.

Give the plants plenty of water and good feeding with a tomato fertilizer, available at your nursery. Keep the plants growing continuously so you have a good harvest. Fertilize first about a week after you put plants in permanent pots of soil, and again in about 2 weeks. While plants are producing fruit, fertilize every week.

Pollinate tomato blossoms by shaking the plant. New blossoms open daily over a long period of time. Keep tomatoes at temperatures above 60° F. at night or they might not set fruit. Very warm temperatures, over 95° F., will affect them adversely too, so shelter plants from extreme sun on very hot days.

Thin tomato plants by removing the small suckers as they form. These are the tiny first two or three leaves that appear between the main stem and the foliage. Depending upon the variety, tomatoes should bear within 70 to 80 days after seed planting.

There are many varieties available, including Gardener's Delight, Hybrid Patio, Small Fry, Sparten Red, and Tiny Tim.

Avocados and Pineapples

Once you have the vegetables growing, you'll probably also want to try succulent fruits. So you'll hastily plant an avocado pit or a pineapple top. Well, don't be misled. Each will produce a fine house plant, but don't expect fruit. But these are throw-away items anyway, so why not use them as decorative kitchen plants?

Everyone seems to love growing avocados. Indeed, there are several good books devoted specifically to the subject. To start avocados, clean the pit and place the larger part of the pit in a jar or glass of water. You can use the old 4-toothpick method (one at each side of the pit) to keep it propped up. Or start the pit in sand or vermiculite and transplant later. Try to keep the avocado plant pinched back at the beginning so it'll be bushy rather than just a beanstalk.

Even though this tropical denizen does make a somewhat nice, if familiar, houseplant, there are other things from the kitchen you can grow, including pineapple. Instead of paying $15 for *Ananas comosus* (the pineapple plant), start your own. It's simple. Remove the leafy top with a twist of the hand; put the top in sand in a shallow dish. Keep it moist, and when roots start (and you will see them), transplant the top into fresh soil in a larger container. Soon green leaves will start sprouting, and you'll have a lovely yet tough kitchen plant.

CHAPTER TEN

Condominium and Mobile Home Gardens

A condominium is a multitype dwelling in which homeowners own their units and the land directly underneath and, with other owners, have joint ownership of all property; for example, walkways and parking areas. The landscaping around the complex is predetermined, but many condominium townhouses have a backyard or patio area that has been walled off for privacy, and the apartment units usually have balconies that can be used for gardening. In either case, these areas afford the homeowner a place to garden at leisure.

Although the patio or allotted garden area is already walled or fenced, homeowners must supply all soil and plant materials and do their own gardens or outdoor rooms. But the patio garden gives greenery and offers low maintenance and care, and it can be landscaped in several different ways, depending upon the personal taste of the owner and the dictates of money.

Balconies for gardening are usually small, but recently builders have enlarged these areas; here is a perfect place to do container gardening. Growing plants in tubs and boxes is an easy way to have a few plants do a lot for you, and, again, care is minimum.

THE PATIO GARDEN

A patio or terrace in the home needs planning and design because even if it is used for only a few months in the year, it serves as another room. Before deciding what and where to plant, decide what it will be. The size and your personal needs will dictate what kind of outdoor living area to have. It can be a simple exposed patio, with plants adjacent to the home to provide a handsome

This condominium garden has sparse plantings but enough greenery to excellently frame the unit. (Photo by Joyce Wilson)

picture and make the room look larger. If you enjoy outdoor cookery and dining, it can be a fully enclosed or partially roofed terrace near the dining room or the kitchen. A terrace can also be a walled area off the bedroom, decorated with flowering plants.

Pavings

The first consideration for the patio is the floor; walls (if not already in place) and ceilings (canopies, arbors, overhangs) can be built later. Look at all types of pavings at material supply yards and garden centers before making a decision. Industry offers a wide selection for outdoor flooring materials. Choose carefully; select a paving that is in character with your home. A patio floor may be concrete, but it can also be brick or flagstone for a dramatic picture or tile for long-lasting beauty.

Before making your final decision about the patio floor, ask yourself some questions.

1. Will the paving withstand weather and wear?
2. Will it be easy to maintain?
3. Is the floor comfortable to walk on? Is it so rough that it might injure children's knees?
4. Does water sink through the paving, or does it flow off in sheets, making it slippery?
5. Should the paving be light in color or dark? Light paving creates a glare; dark paving stores up heat. And, finally, think about the cost and the installation fee.

Concrete—Concrete may not be as handsome as some other pavings, but it is a durable, low-cost, and very permanent surface. It is easy to clean, and if you object to its cold feeling, mix it with color or cover it with paint or dye the top layer with liquid, which will seep deeply into the pores of the concrete. The concrete can also be rough or textured.

An aggregate floor is another idea. It is made of concrete that has small stones on the surface. The textured finish is handsome and blends with plantings and lawns. The uneven texture breaks the monotony of a large area of paving, especially when it is framed with wood grids. The pebbly surface of aggregate concrete also eliminates glare and guarantees sure traction in wet weather. And when this paving collects dirt—as it will—it is easy to clean with a strong hosing.

A slick or hard finish is made by moving a steel trowel over the surface when it is partially hardened. Do the first troweling lightly, just enough to smooth the float texture. Then trowel again with more pressure. This floor is slick and somewhat uninteresting.

The wood-float method leaves a floor smooth but not shiny. It is done with the mason's wood trowel (float).

The broom finish gives an interesting texture. It is made by brushing the slightly hardened concrete with a push broom.

Brick—Brick is the most popular paving material; it is difficult to commit a serious error when paving with it. By using the simple method of brick on sand it is easy to take up the section and re-lay it if the first attempt is not pleasing or accurate.

Brick comes in a variety of earthy colors that look good outdoors and impart a pleasant contrast in texture. There are rough- and smooth-surfaced brick, glazed or unglazed. Other shapes are available too: hexagon, octagon, fleur-de-lis. Because the units are small, they never steal the show, and they stay in scale with even the smallest foliage display.

There are many kinds of brick, but the best ones for patios are smooth-surfaced or rough-textured common brick. Face brick, including Roman and paving brick, is easier to work with and less expensive than slick brick. Common brick is usually available with pit marks on the surface. Sand-mold brick is smooth-textured and slightly larger on one face than on the other, and clinker brick has irregularities on the surface. If you can, select hard-burned rather than green brick. It should be dark red in color rather than salmon, which indicates an underburned process and less durability. Used bricks or colored ones are fine too. When you select the brick flooring be sure the dealer has a sufficient quantity to complete the area because there is usually some dimensional variation and color difference in later orders of brick. If you are in a climate where winters are severe, specify SW (severe weathering) brick.

Bricks can be laid in a great variety of patterns—herringbone, basket-weave, running bond, and so on—or combined with squares of grass or cinders in endless designs. For large areas, choose the herringbone pattern; smaller patios look best with running bond or basket-weave designs. Or break the large area by fitting bricks into redwood or cedar grid patterns. Bricks can also be set in mortar, but this is usually a job for the professional bricklayer.

Planning and Planting

You will find that a small condominium patio garden not only delights the eye, but also means minimal gardening to keep you active and to create your own private Eden. In condominium living the tendency to arrange many buildings in a cluster often coaxes the owner to provide greenery for the eye and satisfaction for the soul. And walled patio gardening is a delight to do. As your own special place, it is worth its space in gold.

As mentioned, a hard surface floor most likely will already have been installed by the contractor. If possible, and you get there first, have him leave planting pockets for plants. This breaks the monotony of a solid paved area, and plants look good used in this way because they seem to belong rather than just being placed. Use two large planting pockets (for trees, perhaps) as accents, and place smaller planter beds along one wall for perennials and annuals. You do want plants in the patio, of course, but you do not want a jungle here because you will often use the patio as an extra room for entertaining. So a few specimen types, a minimum of shrubbery, and a flower bed are really all that is required.

Plan the private garden with consideration of line and detail. In the outdoors, where there is a natural background, you can get away with a few mistakes, but not here. You will be working in a confined area, so you need to have every plant perfect and superbly chosen. Do search for that perfect olive tree with gnarled branches and sweeping graceful lines as an accent, and do select full bushy shrubs that will add low horizontal thrust to the scene. Provide seasonal color with perennials and annuals in suitable planters or in the ground or spaces that have been left open in the paved area. Later you can add some stunning potted plant specimens to be used outdoors in good weather and indoors in cold weather to provide decoration.

A place to sit, some benches, and perhaps some statuary can transform the condominium garden into a visual treat you can be proud of, and taking care of the plants will entail only a few hours a week. If the patio area of your condominium is already paved, you will be forced to use container plants unless you want to dig up some paving. Plants in containers—and almost any plant can be grown in a pot for some time—will allow you to decorate the area a little at a time. Select ornamental tubs and boxes (there are dozens now at suppliers) and choose small, graceful trees. Grow bulbs and perennials and some annuals in planter boxes, which can be made from redwood for that important seasonal color. Shrubs in containers will look their best trimmed and pruned frequently, so be aware of this when planning the container garden. Once again, house plants and trees of all kinds can be used in the patio in handsome tubs when weather permits and returned indoors for winter decoration.

Use line and balance within your patio, selecting vertical plants as well as low massing horizontal ones to balance the scene. For the best results, group planters and tubs together—say three tubs to an area—so you can provide a good display rather than a lone tub that will give a spotty effect. Groups of six or ten small pots with plants are handsome. Search out the really ornamental urns and jardinieres rather than the usual wooden ones. A certain amount of decorative flair is needed to make the patio garden a stellar one.

Caring for your plants in the patio garden is merely a question of sufficient watering and moderate feeding. Plants in tubs and boxes will need more water than those directly in the ground, and, in all cases, a sensible feeding and grooming program will keep everything in top shape.

MOBILE HOMES

Mobile homes are apt to be confused with a trailer or camper. Actually, they are small factory-built houses delivered to a site. The fact that they do have wheels to get them to the site has confused the issue somewhat. Once on the property, the mobile

A mobile home garden can be quite desirable, as seen here. This uses easy maintenance stone and chipped fir bark for cover. (Photo by Joyce Wilson)

home is placed on a pier foundation and connected to water and electrical systems; there the home stays until the owner decides to leave, in which case wheels are attached and the home is moved somewhere else. Portability is its asset, and these mobile homes can be as large as 1,500 square feet, the size of an average house.

As vacation retreats, mobile homes serve a definite purpose. Each year you can choose your own location and enjoy a multitude of climates. The major problem with mobile homes is that they are not welcome everywhere because, even though they may be lovely outside and inside, once set on a piece of land they appear out of place.

Some kind of temporary or permanent landscaping is necessary to make the mobile home visually acceptable. At first this may seem a chore, but one of my assistants who has a mobile home proved to me it is possible to transform these homes on wheels into a lovely picture. In a few months time she added a small grass area, pebbled paths, and some container plants. Approaching her home, one does feel it is a home and not just a structure placed on a hunk of land.

A small lawn area around the sides and front of a mobile home softens the somewhat severe appearance. Such a small expanse of lawn does not cost much and can be accomplished in a relatively short time. Stones and pebbles (other inexpensive materials) can also work wonders in providing a softening effect for the home. And rather than put plants into the ground, they can be in containers so they can be moved at will. Such landscaping is hardly complete, but it offers enough greenery to make the total scene attractive.

For privacy, hedges on each side of the mobile home may be a sound idea even though these must be in the ground. The cost, about $40, will be well worth the expenditure. Small window boxes and planters are other added touches that can bring greenery to the mobile home situation.

Planning and Planting

The best approach to the planning of the mobile home garden is to frame the house on three sides; make it an entity in itself. Plants can do the job for you better than anything else. Plants also provide privacy in such situations. Do not be afraid to use some tall hedge shrubs and an occasional small tree to give dimension to the site.

Container gardening again comes to the rescue, and you can grow almost any plant you want in this manner. Keep the plan simple but attractive. Too many plants will require too much care and make the site seem forced rather than natural. But a few well-chosen plants in specific areas, especially corners near the mobile home, can add great beauty.

Pebble walks and stone areas are other ways of providing attractiveness for the mobile home without adding work to your daily schedule. Do not try to have everything on the mobile home site; use well-chosen plants that you like.

Any vacation place, as we have shown throughout this book, can become beautiful with carefully selected plants that provide greenery and color and make the vacation or second home a place you will want to come to. Barren sites are hardly handsome, so pitch in with soil and plants and you will be amazed at what you can accomplish in a short time without much cost or labor.

Greenery surrounds this mobile home and the result is a very pleasant garden. (Photo by Joyce Wilson)

CHAPTER ELEVEN

Greenhouses

G reenhouses are not necessary for gardening prowess, but they are certainly a convenience, especially for the person who can't work outdoors too much or bend or stoop a great deal. Commercial greenhouses are available in many styles, and some of the smaller models can certainly add to and extend your gardening season. But you might want to try to design your own greenhouse, in which case you can plan accordingly and have raised benches to fit your stature, shelves within your reach, and many other arrangements developed just for you. It's a great way to garden year-round because greenhouses are excellent for starting seeds, propagating cuttings, growing flowers and houseplants, and so forth.

A TYPICAL GREENHOUSE

If you decide to get a greenhouse or have one built, study manufacturers' catalogs. See what ideas are good and forget bad ones. Among the commercial greenhouses, the lean-to style (a greenhouse that uses one wall of your house) is the most popular. There are many lean-to models: some need a concrete foundation, but others can be built on a concrete slab. Remember that the greenhouse adjacent to your home has the advantages of providing a pretty winter picture and of being easily accessible from your home. In Chicago, my mornings were always cheerful because the greenhouse adjoined the kitchen. I could enjoy morning coffee while viewing the flowers in their crystal palace as snow and sleet raged outdoors. Quite a comfortable feeling!

If it is impossible to put the greenhouse next to the house, consider a gallery leading from the house to the structure; this is

A small homemade greenhouse can provide owners with many extra hours of pleasurable gardening. (Photo by C. and D. Luckhardt)

like walking through a park arbor, and you never have to worry about inclement weather. Freestanding greenhouses are also available from suppliers. However, they are expensive and never made much sense to me.

A southern exposure is the best location for a greenhouse, but I have also seen lovely glass gardens on the east or west side of a home. Even in a north light you can grow lovely foliage plants, start seedlings, and so forth. In the south or southeast exposure the greenhouse benefits from winter sunlight; an eastern exposure is good because there is morning sun, and the unit that faces west will have bright light and some afternoon sun. Make your greenhouse large enough so you have space to work but not so large that it becomes a burden. A good size is 10 x 18 feet.

YOUR OWN GREENHOUSE

Prefabricated commercial greenhouses come unassembled, so putting them together is your job. Because this can be a complicated chore in spite of the many instruction sheets, planning your own unit and having it built is appealing since it allows you to create special things suited to your personal wants. The information you can garner from greenhouse manufacturers' catalogs will tell you how the basic frame is made—follow this for your own design. Once you have the plan on paper, find a local carpenter who can do the job for you. Get prices and costs, and have him furnish all building materials and hardware. A carpenter is an ingenious man, and once he has a rough sketch of the greenhouse you want to have, he can proceed to work with you on its final design.

GREENHOUSE KNOW-HOW

No matter what kind of gardening you decide to do in your greenhouse—sowing seeds, raising garden plants or houseplants—there are certain conditions you'll have to maintain for the plants:

A homemade greenhouse attached to the home gives the owner ample space to grow fine plants and spend hours of enjoyment. (Photo by C. and D. Luckhardt)

the proper amount of humidity, correct temperatures, ventilation, and so forth.

Humidity

Try to maintain humidity at about 40 to 60 percent for such tropical plants as orchids, ferns, and bromeliads, or for starting seeds. Humidity can be as low as 20 to 30 percent for cacti and succulents. The air will need more moisture as you increase the heat, and on very hot muggy days the humidity should also be high. Naturally, relative humidity will increase at night.

Temperature

Most plants thrive with a daytime temperature of 60° to 75° F. and a 10- to 15-degree drop at night. However, avoid *sudden* temperature changes because they can harm plants. At about 6:00 start to gradually change the evening temperature. The minimum should be reached during the late night hours.

Ventilation

Because most plants need good air circulation (but with a minimum of drafts), open the ventilators during the day, even in very cold weather, to allow some air into the greenhouse. (Make sure the ventilators are opposite the side from which the wind is blowing.) In early spring, the temperatures fluctuate unless you have thermostatic controls, so you may have to open and close vents several times a day. Consider carefully the many different types of heating for the greenhouse: hot water, warm air, electric, and gas. You may have to call in a professional to recommend the best system for the greenhouse.

Watering

Too much shade and moisture can encourage fungus diseases on plants. Soil should be evenly moist for most plants, although resting ones (see below) need a somewhat drier soil. Mist plants early in the morning so the sun can dry them quickly.

A greenhouse in winter provides excellent protection for plants.

The total cost of this makeshift greenhouse was under $1000. (Photo by author)

Resting Plants

This is a vital part of successful plant culture because most plants need a period of rest (lower temperatures and less water) at some time of the year. Generally, the resting time occurs after blooming. If your greenhouse is full of leaves instead of flowers, your plants aren't getting proper resting periods. Some part of the greenhouse will naturally have lower temperatures; this is the place to put resting plants.

Shading

Shading is generally applied in early spring and removed in fall. You can use shading paint or devise other means to protect plants from hot direct sun, which harms them. Roller blinds and trellises over the greenhouse that can easily be removed in winter are some of the other ways of shading plants.

Protection from Insects

Keep a vigilant lookout for insects. When you see them, take immediate steps to eliminate them, because once insects have a foothold, they are difficult to eradicate. Use *only botanical sprays* when dealing with insects; poisonous chemicals are not necessary in the home greenhouse and should be avoided.

General List of Plants

The following list of trees, shrubs, and perennials is to help you determine which plants need a lot of water (wet soil conditions) and which require little water (dry soil conditions).

FOR WET SOIL CONDITIONS

Trees, Deciduous

Acer rubrum
  (red maple)
Alnus glutinosa
  (black alder)
Betula populifolia
  (gray birch)
Gleditsia aquatica
  (water locust)
Liquidambar styraciflua
  (sweet gum)

Platanus occidentalis
  (buttonwood)
Quercus palustris
  (pin oak)
Salix alba
  (white willow)
Tilia americana
  (American linden)

Trees, Evergreen

Abies balsamea
  (balsam fir)
Thuja occidentalis
  (arborvitae)

Tsuga canadensis
  (hemlock)

Shrubs

Alnus (various)
  (alders)

Amelanchier canadensis
  (shadblow serviceberry)

Andromeda species
  (andromeda)

Aronia arbutifolia
  (red chokeberry)

Calluna vulgaris
  (heather)

Clethra alnifolia
  (summer sweet)

Cornus alba
  (tatarian dogwood)

Cornus sanguinea
  (bloodtwig dogwood)

Cornus stolonifera
  (red osier)

Hypericum densiflorum
  (dense hypericum)

Ilex glabra
  (inkberry)

Ilex verticillata
  (winterberry)

Kalmia angustifolia
  (sheep laurel)

Ligustrum amurense
  (amur privet)

Pieris floribunda
  (mountain andromeda)

Rhododendron (various)
  (rhododendron)

Sabal minor
  (dwarf palmetto)

Salix (various)
  (willow)

Spiraea menziesii
  (spirea)

Spiraea tomentosa

Vaccinium corymbosum
  (highbush blueberry)

Viburnum alnifolium
  (hobblebush)

Viburnum cassinoides

Viburnum dentatum
  (arrowwood)

Viburnum lentago
  (nannyberry)

Viburnum sieboldii
  (siebold viburnum)

Perennials

Arundo 'Donax'
  (giant reed)
Asclepias incarnata
  (swamp milkweed)
Caltha palustris
  (marsh marigold)
Equisetum hyemale
  (horsetail)
Gentiana asclepiadea
  (willow gentian)
Helenium (various)
  (Helen's flower)
Hibiscus moscheutos
  (swamp rose mallow)
Iris pseudacorus
  (yellow flag)

Iris veriscolor
  (blue flag)
Lobelia cardinalis
  (cardinal flower)
Lythrum (various)
  (loosestrife)
Monarda didyma
  (bee balm)
Myosotis scorpioides
  (true forget-me-not)
Oenothera (various)
  (evening primrose)
Sarracenia purpurea
  (pitcher plants)
Saxifraga (various)
  (saxifrage)
Vinca
  (periwinkle)

FOR DRY SOIL CONDITIONS

Trees, Deciduous

Acer ginnala
  (Amur maple)
Acer tataricum
  (tatarian maple)
Ailanthus altissima
  (tree of heaven)
Betula pendula
  (European birch)

Betula populifolia
  (gray birch)
Carya glabra
  (pignut)
Cotinus coggygria
  (smoke tree)
Populus alba
  (white poplar)

Populus tremuloides
   (quaking aspen)
Prunus cerasus
   (sour cherry)
Prunus serotina
   (black cherry)

Quercus suber
   (cork oak)
Robinia pseudoacacia
   (black locust)

Trees, Evergreen

Juniperus chinensis
   (Chinese juniper)
Juniperus virginiana
   (eastern red cedar)
Picea abies (P. excelsa)
   (Norway spruce)
Picea alba (P. glauca)
   (Canadian spruce)

Pinus mugo
   (Swiss mountain pine)
Pinus rigida
   (pitch pine)
Pinus strobus
   (white pine)
Pinus sylvestris
   (Scots pine)

Shrubs

Arctostaphylos uva-ursi
   (bearberry)
Arubtus unedo
   (strawberry tree)
Berberis (several)
   (barberry)
Betula glandulosa
Betula nana
Buddleia alternifolia
   (fountain buddleia)
Ceanothus americanus
   (New Jersey tea)
Cotoneaster
   (cotoneaster)

Cytisus
   (broom)
Elaeagnus angustifolia
   (Russian olive)
Euonymus japonica
   (evergreen euonymus)
Genista tinctoria
   (dyer's greenwood)
Hamamelis virginiana
   (common witch hazel)
Hypericum
   (shrubby Saint-John's-wort)
Juniperus communis
   (juniper)

Juniperus horizontalis
  (creeping juniper)
Kolkwitzia amabilis
  (beauty bush)
Ligustrum vulgare
  (common privet)
Nerium oleander
  (oleander)
Pittosporum tobira
  (Japanese pittosporum)
Potentilla fruticosa
  (cinquefoil)
Prunus besseyi
  (western sand cherry)
Prunus maritima
  (beach plum)
Pyracantha coccinea
  (scarlet firethorn)
Raphiolepis umbellata
  (hawthorn)

Rhamnus alaternus
Rhamnus frangula
  (alder buckthorn)
Rhus (various)
  (sumac)
Robinia hispida
  (rose acacia)
Robinia pseudoacacia
  (black locust)
Robinia viscosa
  (clammy locust)
Rosa (various)
  (rose)
Salix species
  (willow)
Tamarix species
  (tamarix)
Viburnum lantana
  (wayfaring tree)
Viburnum lentago
  (nannyberry)

Perennials

Achillea (various)
  (yarrow)
Ajuga reptans
  (carpet bugle)
Anthemis tinctoria
  (golden marguerite)
Artemisia pycnocephala
Asclepias tuberosa
  (butterfly weed)

Aster novae-angliae
  (New England aster)
Callirhoe involucrata
  (poppy mallow)
Cerastium tomentosum
  (snow-in-summer)
Coreopsis grandiflora
  (tickseed)

Dianthus (various)
(pinks)
Echinops exaltatus
(globe thistle)
Echium
Gazania hybrids
Geranium grandiflorum
(cranesbill)
Gypsophila paniculata
(baby's breath)
Helianthus (various)
(sunflower)
Limonium latifolium
(statice, sea lavender)

Papaver nudicaule
(Iceland poppy)
Phlox subulata
(moss pink)
Potentilla atrosanguinea
(cinquefoil)
Rudbeckia hirta
(coneflower)
Veronica (various)
(speedwell)
Yucca filamentosa
(Adam's needle)